Gaining Ground in Illinois

Gaining Ground
in Illinois

Welfare Reform and
Person-Centered
Policy Analysis

Dan A. Lewis

NORTHERN ILLINOIS UNIVERSITY PRESS

DeKalb

© 2010 by Northern Illinois University Press

Published by the Northern Illinois University Press, DeKalb, Illinois 60115

Manufactured in the United States using postconsumer-recycled, acid-free paper.

All Rights Reserved

Design by Shaun Allshouse

Library of Congress Cataloging-in-Publication Data

Lewis, Dan A.

  Gaining ground in Illinois: welfare reform and person-centered policy analysis /
Dan A. Lewis.

     p. cm.

  Includes bibliographical references and index.

  ISBN 978-0-87580-627-3 (pbk.: alk. paper)

1. Public welfare—Illinois. 2. Public welfare—United States. 3. Poor—Services for—
Government policy—Illinois. I. Title.

  HV98.I15L49 2010

   362.5′56109773—dc22

                                   2009036802

For Stephanie,

who has been at my side through thick and thin

and whose love keeps me going.

Contents

Acknowledgments   ix

SECTION 1—Welfare Reform in Political and Ideological Perspective in Illinois and Nationally

1—Beyond Left and Right and the Problem of Welfare Reform   5

2—Making the Words Flesh
  Welfare Reform in the Illinois Political Culture   15

3—The Illinois Families Study   33

SECTION 2—Person-Centered Characteristics that Influence the Outcomes of Welfare Reform

4—Two Worlds of Welfare
  Overview of Welfare Caseload Trends in Illinois   49

5—Working and Earning After Welfare Reform   66

6—Depression and Welfare   77

7—How the Children Fare   87

SECTION 3—Policy Factors Influencing the Poor in Illinois

8—Sanctions
  Do They Help or Hurt the Poor?   97

9—Did Welfare Reform Launch the Poor into Better Neighborhoods?   110

10—Assessing the Results and Moving Forward   123

Appendix A—*Springfield Data Collection*   131
Appendix B—*Background on the IFS Qualitative Sample*   133
Notes   139
References   143
Index   155

Acknowledgments

This book was a decade in the making. There are contributions from over a dozen people: graduate students, undergraduates, and colleagues. Each chapter has contributions from others, and all the chapters were based on previously written articles, some published and others not. I will list the contributors to each chapter below. This book was also supported by over ten grants from various foundations and government agencies. That support was key to getting the work done. The generosity of these funders made the research possible. Needless to say, but I will say it anyway, the views expressed in these pages do not represent the positions of the funding agencies or the contributors to the earlier works that have been incorporated here. The modifications made and the conclusions drawn are solely the responsibility of the author.

I want to make special mention of the Woods Charitable Trust, the MacArthur Foundation, and the Joyce Foundation for their early support of the project. Although the State of Illinois was only a reluctant funder of the effort, I would like to acknowledge the important contribution of Dave Gruenenfelder of the Illinois Department of Human Services, who shepherded the project through its early years with grace and intelligence. John Bouman, who now runs the Sargent Shriver Center for Poverty Law, was very important to the project this book reports on, and his sound counsel throughout the effort was extremely important to me. I was also blessed with three project managers over the life of the University Consortium on Welfare Reform whose abilities and personalities made for the success of the project. Kristin Shook Slack, Amy Stevens, and Laura Amsden all did a splendid job. Each contributed to this book in myriad ways, drafting parts of our reports to the Illinois legislature, and in Kristi's case, coauthoring one of the articles that became the basis of a chapter. I would also like to recognize the contributions of the faculty members from other universities who constituted the University Consortium on

Welfare Reform: Paul Kleppner from Northern Illinois University; Jim Lewis, who was then associated with Roosevelt University; Stephanie Riger from the University of Illinois at Chicago; and Robert Goerge from the University of Chicago. The Consortium planned the overall design of the project and gave valuable suggestions throughout the six years the project was operating. I also want to acknowledge the contribution of the Metropolitan Chicago Information Center (MCIC) and in particular Patricia Gross. This organization was charged with the data collection for the Illinois Families Study (IFS), the panel study of welfare recipients that formed the backbone of the research reported in this book. Patricia oversaw the data collection and data preparation, and I am deeply appreciative of her fine work as well as that of her colleagues. Robert Goerge also deserves thanks for his oversight of the administrative data presented in this book. He and his team at Chapin Hall did a first-rate job, and I am very thankful. I also want to thank Bruce Nelson, who oversaw the collection of the qualitative data presented here and worked very hard to organize that material.

The book was improved by the editorial assistance of Barbara Ray, who worked with me for more than a year, improving my prose and adding immensely to the final product. Now to the contributors to this book:

Chapter 1: Parts of this chapter first appeared in *Policy Analysis Methods*, edited by Stuart S. Nagel and published in 1999 by Nova Science Publishers. The original essay was coauthored by Shadd Maruna and was entitled *Person Centered Policy Analysis*.

Chapter 2: Parts of this chapter first appeared as an essay in *Families, Poverty and Welfare Reform* (1999) edited by Lawrence B. Joseph. That essay was coauthored by Christine C. George and Deborah Puntenney, and was titled "Welfare Reform Efforts in Illinois." I would also like to acknowledge and thank two undergraduates who did their honors theses under my supervision and whose work contributed to this chapter, Elissa Koch and Janice Law. Christine George did an excellent dissertation (2001) that I supervised, and some of the interviews she did for it were used in this chapter. Finally, Bruce Nelson, Irene Carvalho, and I wrote an unpublished paper, *Identity, Work and Welfare Reform: A Qualitative Analysis*, which formed the basis of some of the analysis presented.

Chapter 3: Based on the fourth annual report of the Illinois Families Study, July 2004. Special thanks to Kristen Shook Slack, University of Wisconsin–Madison; Bong Joo Lee, University of Chicago, now at Seoul National University; Paul Kleppner, Northern Illinois University; James Lewis, Roosevelt University; Stephanie Riger, University of Illinois at Chicago; and Robert Goerge, Chapin Hall Center for Children, University of Chicago. The quotes from various study participants are drawn throughout the book from our interviews with Illinois women. Special thanks to the more than 1,000 women who were willing to share their lives with us, and to Bruce Nelson for organizing the quotes.

Chapter 4: Based on the fourth annual report of the Illinois Families Study, July 2004. Special thanks to Kristen Shook Slack, University of Wisconsin–Madison; Bong Joo Lee, University of Chicago, now at Seoul National University; Paul Kleppner, Northern Illinois University; James Lewis, Roosevelt University; Stephanie Riger, University of Illinois at Chicago; and Robert Goerge, Chapin Hall Center for Children, University of Chicago. The quotes from various study participants are drawn throughout the book from our interviews with Illinois women.

Chapter 5: Based on work done with Spyros Konstantopoulos, School of Education and Social Policy, Northwestern University, and Lisa Altenbernd, doctoral candidate, at the School of Education and Social Policy, Northwestern University.

Chapter 6: Based on and adapted from work done with Bong Joo Lee, Seoul National University, and Lisa Altenbernd, doctoral candidate, Institute for Policy Research, Northwestern University. An earlier version of this chapter was originally published by Dan A. Lewis, Bong Joo Lee, and Lisa Altenbernd, "Depression and Welfare Reform: From Barriers to Inclusion," *Journal of Community Psychology* 34(4) (2005): 415–33.

Chapter 7: Adapted from work done with Amber Stitziel Pareja, Northwestern University: "Welfare Reform and Academic Achievement: What Happens to Poor Children's Test Scores When Their Parents Go to Work?," an unpublished manuscript, and "The Effect of Parental Employment on Children's Academic Achievement in the Context of Welfare Reform," a paper presented at the American Sociological Society Annual Meeting in 2006. Amber also completed a dissertation based on the data collected on the children in the IFS sample. I wish to acknowledge her hard work, which made this chapter possible.

Chapter 8: This chapter appeared in an earlier version in the *Social Service Review* 78(3) (September 2004). The article was entitled "Are Welfare Sanctions Working as Intended? Welfare Receipt, Work Activity, and Material Hardship among TANF Recipient Families." It was coauthored with Bong Joo Lee and Kristen S. Slack.

Chapter 9: This chapter appeared in an earlier version in Urban Affairs Review 43(2) (November 2007). The article was entitled "Moving Up and Moving Out? Economic and Residential Mobility in Low-Income Chicago Families." It was coauthored with Vandna Sinha.

Chapter 10: This chapter draws a bit from a 1998 article, "Person-centered Policy Analysis," *Research in Public Policy Analysis and Management* 9: 213–30. It was coauthored by Shadd Maruna.

Appendix B was written with the assistance of Irene Carvahlo and Bruce Nelson of the Institute for Policy Research at Northwestern University.

The funders of the project include

John D. and Catherine T. MacArthur Foundation

Joyce Foundation

Woods Charitable Trust

Searle Foundation

Polk Brothers Foundation U.S. Department of Education

Annie E. Casey Foundation

Administration for Children and Families, U.S. Department of Health and Human Services

Board of Higher Education, State of Illinois

Chicago Community Trust

Lindsay Monte, Rachel Zanders, and Alice Murray provided some last-minute help in getting the final manuscript out the electronic door. I appreciate their efforts. Lastly, the support I have received from the Institute for Policy Research at Northwestern University over my entire career has been essential to whatever I have accomplished. It is much appreciated.

Gaining Ground in Illinois

SECTION 1

Welfare Reform in Political and

Ideological Perspective in

Illinois and Nationally

Beyond Left and Right and the Problem of Welfare Reform

ON JULY 8, 1997, the State of Illinois passed an act that was designed to assess the impact of the country's new federal welfare law (PRWORA) on the poor of Illinois. Illinois's Welfare Reform Research and Accountability Act was signed into law by the Republican governor after being passed by the Democratic-controlled Illinois House of Representatives and the Republican-controlled Illinois State Senate. The new Illinois law required the state to find an independent scholar to study the impact of the new welfare reform on the poor of Illinois and report back to the General Assembly. The Illinois law was crafted and introduced into the State Senate by a young state senator from Chicago named Barack Obama. That law gave birth to the book you are about to read. Obama felt that a sound piece of research assessing how the new federal welfare law affected the poor of Illinois would give lawmakers a way to come together and improve the law and the lives of the poor. Obama, as we all came to realize in the presidential campaign of 2008, argued that the conventional categories of left and right have kept us from working together to solve pressing problems. Ideology was getting in the way of comity and progress. Ideology was blinding us to what we had in common and literally "seeing" the problems clearly. Welfare reform is a perfect example of what Obama was and is talking about. The 1996 federal law sprang from the Republican Party's ability to win control of the U.S. House of Representatives in 1994. They already controlled the U.S. Senate at that time. Liberals and conservatives had been battling for at least twenty-five years over what to do about welfare (usually defined as the Aid to Families with Dependent Children program, or AFDC). The 1996 Personal Responsibility Work Opportunity Reconciliation Act (PRWORA) signaled the victory of the conservatives. AFDC was to be abolished along with the entitlement to support that had been guaranteed by the earlier program. The battle over that legislation was vicious and unremitting (Haskins, 2006; Weaver, 2000). Many liberals thought President Clinton's signing of the bill was "the worst thing he had done" (Edelman, 1997), and many liberal scholars predicted dire consequences for the poor when the law went into effect. Politicians and scholars on the right saw PRWORA as a, if not the, most important challenge to the welfare state in the last fifty years. They saw the new law transforming the lives of the poor for the better. There was little room for compromise between the way liberals and conservatives saw the causes of extreme poverty and the proposed remedies. Politics played vastly different roles in these perspectives, which defined the welfare recipient herself differently. We will outline these differences in some detail and then provide a new orientation built on our analysis of welfare recipients that hopefully blends the different viewpoints, transcends the ideological battles of the past, and does a better job of illuminating the lives of the poor and what can be done to improve the situation.

PRWORA reflected a prescription for change that was about how wrong the liberals were in their analysis of the welfare issue. The liberals were so sure the conservatives were wrong that they could not see how PRWORA would do anything but cause more problems for the poor. Both sides talked and analyzed in a race to make points and justify basic assumptions about the welfare state and human nature. Obama hoped that, at least in Illinois, reason based on empirical research could shift the debate to what we know about how policy affected people. Ideology could be trumped by careful analysis, and we could move to a point of making policy based on evidence.

As the reader will see in the pages to come, the law did transform the lives of the poor, but not in the ways either side had predicted. Indeed, we will propose a third way to look at the problem that hopefully elevates the discussion and gives us a better understanding of the lives of the poor and what policies would lead to improvements. By looking at the impact of the new law on the lives of welfare recipients, we can extend Obama's insight about moving beyond the tired battles of left and right in the political realm to the policy analysis arena. It is true that the conservative approach brought us a new world in which welfare as we knew it is gone. That may have been the right's intent, but the demise of AFDC has not made the poor disappear. Conservatives wanted a world in which the government was out of our business (at least, the poor's business). In their antipathy to the liberal welfare state, they blamed that state for the behaviors of the poor and did not "see" that in the absence of AFDC, there would still be factors that would produce poverty. The conservative paradigm did not anticipate the negative side of reform. Removing the old AFDC system and requiring the poor to fend for themselves in the labor market was, as we shall see in the pages that follow, not a panacea. Those people with less human capital were not equipped to compete for work at low-paying jobs. They now live in the shadow land between family and state. With the removal of welfare as we knew it, a new world of dependency has emerged, one that costs the taxpayer less in the short run but leaves many of the poor relegated to a shadow world hidden between the state and the market.

For conservatives, AFDC mattered considerably in terms of economic outcomes. That program imprisoned the poor in a life outside the mainstream. For conservatives, labor market participation enabled rather than retarded improvement. Freed of traditional welfare programs, most citizens would find work and improve their economic status. The pressure of the market stimulates progress for the poor. Individual differences between people do matter, and those with the right motivations and personality will and should do better than those without those traits. A world without welfare is a better world for the poor in the conservative paradigm.

Where did the liberals go wrong? Leaving aside the obvious political mistakes that were made and the general move to the right in public opinion, they failed to take welfare policy seriously as a socializing agent. They saw human nature in optimistic, homogeneous terms, avoiding differences between people (especially the influence of race) and the broader impact of state action on the poor. They looked to economic factors, wages, and jobs as the common denominator of poverty and missed the importance in a democracy of political influences on human development. Faced with a challenge to the very existence of the welfare state and the foundation upon which it rests, the liberals have not mounted a successful counteroffensive. The issue here is not to try to go back to the now discredited world of big federal programs, but rather to link environment to behavior in ways that counteract the negative consequences of the conservative vision while preserving the gains that this vision produced. Liberal thought assumes that the important questions are those of method and technique, not underlying principle and premise. Better studies did not lead to more credibility with either the public or elites.

The link between the poor woman and her political environment is made explicit in the 1996 welfare reforms. Welfare reform signaled a profound change in the stance of the United States government and public toward the poor, one that reinforced individual accountability and defined government programs as a barrier to economic inclusion. By replacing the old system of guaranteed cash assistance with a new system of work requirements and time limits, the Personal Responsibility and Work Opportunity Reconciliation Act sent a strong message to low-income citizens that government assistance was no longer a right of citizenship, but was only temporary and had to be earned by working. But the inclusion triggered by the welfare reform was, as we shall show, no panacea for poverty. Indeed, it is clear that one of the fundamental differences between approaches to welfare policy in the debates prior to PRWORA was the extent to which government policy was believed to have a substantive impact on individual behavior. The conservative case made a compelling argument for reform on the basis of the view that the policies founded by FDR and expanded during the Great Society era had created the bad behaviors that had come to be associated with poverty: primarily, single motherhood and unemployment. Liberal welfare policies shaped the individual in ways that had a profound effect. As the increasing welfare rolls and rapid growth of single-parent families following the Great Society reforms showed, the wrong set of policies had been put in place. The solution? Remove those wrong policies to remove the wrong behavior. Regardless of whether the conservatives were correct in attributing poverty rates and single motherhood to welfare policy, they were certainly convincing.

We propose to go beyond the liberal-conservative dialectic and introduce a new way of seeing how poverty and policy interact. It will mean understanding the emotions and experiences of the people involved. It will mean changing the subject—from programs to persons. Both liberals and conservatives saw individuals reacting to pressures from either government programs (the conservatives) or labor markets (the liberals). We put the person, her character and coping strategies, first. This shift will involve talking to the individuals who are described in our data, collecting their stories, and understanding how these self-understandings both shape and are shaped by their personal circumstances. For it is the person that decides whether to work or not and how to make sense of the pressures she faces. Criminology has a long history of using such person-centered methods. Discussing his life history of the "Jack-Roller," for instance, Shaw (1929, p. 6) writes, "So far as we have been able to determine as yet, the best way to investigate the inner world of the person is through a study of himself through a life-history." Theorists such as Shaw (1930), Becker (1966), and Sykes & Matza (1957) laid the groundwork for the type of contemporary qualitative analysis being done by criminologists such as Canter (1994), Katz (1988), Sampson & Laub (1992, 1993), and Toch (1987). All take seriously criminal offenders' personal understandings of their behavior, and use life history data to present a picture of the "whole person" in their deviance studies. Scott & Lyman (1968) even argue that stories are directly connected to behavior such as crime that is outside of socially approved boundaries. They write, "Since it is with respect to deviant behavior that we call for accounts, the study of deviance and the study of accounts are intrinsically related, and a clarification of accounts will constitute a clarification of deviant phenomena" (p. 62).

It is this approach that we want to extend to poverty and welfare studies. To be sure, there is a rich tradition of qualitative research in the contemporary study of poverty and welfare. Rainwater (1970) and Stack

(1974) epitomize the best of this tradition with their careful analysis of the behavior of the African American poor. There the focus was on how structural factors shaped the options available to the poor. Much behavior that seemed illogical or self-defeating from a distance took on a more understandable shape when the scholar got closer to the situation and took on the perspective of the poor person. More recently, Edin & Lein (1997) and Duncan, Huston, & Weisner (2007) have used qualitative methods to make sense of how welfare recipients and the urban poor navigated a life with few resources and many demands. These studies have made important contributions to our understanding of the lives of the poor. They focus on the similarities of responses to being poor and not the variations within that poor population. The poor react in uniform ways to common pressures, they would argue, with the suggestion that any one of us would react in a similar fashion. If the structural inequalities could be reduced, the coping strategies we see would disappear. The problem lay with the structures the poor have to deal with rather than the strategies they employ. There is a homogeneity of response that follows from interpreting the behaviors within this socialization framework. The poor assume the roles that their statuses require. While we applaud the focus on the person, we believe we have to find a new path between blaming the victim and blaming the economic system.

Ideally, if we can begin to understand the stories people tell about themselves, we can better anticipate how they will react to various types of treatment and we can better develop policies to meet those needs. Narrative person-centered research can allow policy analysts to better understand why interventions are effective for some individuals and not for others. Human subjects react differently to stimuli based on how events are "perceived and interpreted . . . in line with preexisting and emerging goals" (Toch, 1987). Assuming that individuals have different experiences and personalities, therefore, it makes sense that people would react differently to the same policies. Still, Maltz (1994, p. 457) warns of an implicit assumption of "unimodality" in traditional policy analysis. He suggests that much policy research assumes there is only "one mode of behavior for the entire population under study" and that "a single data set will produce a single pattern that can be characterized by mean values."

If psychology tells us that different people react differently to the same environment, and our programs and program measurements treat everyone the same, it is no wonder that we tend to find weak effects in our research. Maltz (1994, pp. 448–49) writes:

> [S]ome delinquents may be driven by family deficiencies that can be treated by treating the family; others may be driven by peer-related motivations or environmental factors that are amenable to treatment by changing their environment; still others may have deep-rooted psychological or physiological

problems that manifest themselves in violent behavior, that may not even be treatable. Yet, instead of considering these types separately, they are usually grouped together in one regression "model."

He points to a study by Rossi, Berk, & Lenihan (1980) in which the researchers found no significant effects from an experimental program designed to help ex-convicts. Disappointed by their results, they reanalyzed their data and found that while one subgroup used the transitional aid program as an excuse for not working, members of another subgroup were in fact helped by the intervention and even went on to earn more than expected. We have pointed out much the same phenomenon in our welfare sample. A given policy affects people differently, with each individual's behavior shaping the policy's effect, in this case, a decline in welfare rolls. Different persons, however, will react differently on the basis of their perceptions of reality. Individuals who perceive that they have "nothing to lose," for example, will have much higher tolerance for social stigma and public disapproval than the rest of us. As policy researchers, we need to say something about why this is, and how policy can be designed to accommodate this fact. If we are urging agencies to take an individualized, case-based approach with clients, we must provide a way to match strategies to the personal attribution styles people employ. We must do this work in the context of sampling procedures that allow us to generalize our results to the populations—in our case, people on welfare we are trying to understand.

This systematic person-centered strategy is within reach. Some of the preliminary work has been done (Lewis & Maruna, 1998). One option is to study the differences in individuals' identity narrative or life stories. Through such analyses, clusters or divergent subgroups of narrative strategies will emerge, each of which may influence behavior in discernible and predictable ways. Therefore, rather than inappropriately lumping heterogeneous populations together (McCord, 1990; Sampson & Laub, 1992), policy analysts and policy makers can better understand how to match different individuals with different programs. Goffman (1961), for instance, discusses types of "sad tales" or stories meant to account for and explain a person's misfortunes. Sykes & Matza (1957) outline the "techniques of neutralization" delinquents use to absolve themselves of responsibility: denial of injury, denial of the victim, and condemnation of the condemners. Building off Sykes and Matza's framework, Scott & Lyman (1968) provide an extensive discussion and typology of what they call "accounts" or storied explanations of deviant behavior. These include appeals to defeasibility, accidents, or biological drives, as well as scapegoating, justifications, and appeals to loyalties.

Critics contend that the collection of life stories is an unnecessarily cumbersome process. Individuals could just as easily be separated into a typology based on SES, IQ, or some trait measure, with potentially

similar results. Though this may be true, those background var
dispositional traits have their own significant shortcoming
generally stable over time. Therefore, any typology based on these _
offers no substantive information to policy makers about how people can
change. For instance, knowing that a program does not seem to work for
very low-IQ individuals is interesting, but ultimately unhelpful, as efforts
to significantly raise adult IQ levels have been largely unsuccessful. By
collecting the narratives of individuals over time, in different stages of the
life course, policy analysts can better understand how this internal process
of change works.

If policy analysts were to collect and study the life story themes, tones,
and images of the welfare recipients in this way, we would have a better
understanding of how policy can more effectively promote change. After
all, we know that individuals change their behavior. We do not understand
exactly how individuals "go straight," but they do (Moffitt, 1993; Sampson
& Laub, 1992). Studies of narrative identity (for example, Maruna, 1995)
and other broad explorations of personality can provide key clues to this
puzzle and lead to more successful interventions.

Much contemporary research removes individuals from the context
of their lives and reduces them to the sum of the variables measured.
Currie (1993, p. 480) calls this process of "variable-ism" a "simplistic and
ultimately misleading pitting of one variable against others: joblessness
versus economic inequality versus race, and so on, as if these could be
meaningfully separated in the lives of real people in the inner city." Life
histories, unlike means and modes, provide a coherent explanation of
how policies affect people within the context of their life course and
social situation.

Still, subjective interpretations need to be grounded within the
"structural contexts" in which these stories were formed (Groves & Lynch,
1990; Sampson, 1993). Katz (1988) calls this the merging of "phenomenal
foreground" with "social background," and we would suggest that the two
dimensions are highly intertwined. Identity theorists such as Erikson argue
that identity is shaped within the constraints and opportunity structure
of the social world. Rather than stripping individuals of community and
macrohistorical context, therefore, person-centered analysis can inform
both our social and psychological understanding of behavior by illustrating
how the person sees and experiences the environment around her. We will
link the phenomenal foreground to that social and economic background
in the pages to come.

Because stories are highly contextual and contingent on individual
circumstances and life experiences, additional research should address both
how personal narratives shape behavioral patterns, and how situations shape
personal narratives. Researchers should ask how different types of work, life
experiences, or various forms of counseling and education affect the stories

people tell about themselves. Finally, and most obviously, person-centered research can bring policy analysts closer to the populations we are studying. Increasingly, policy researchers do not know the individuals who make up our data. We know a great deal about their statistics, of course. We know the mean income level of an experimental sample before and after some intervention and how it compares to the control group's mean according to the t test. Although the importance of this knowledge should not be underestimated, we are running the risk of losing touch with the stories and lives of the individuals we are trying to understand (Lewis, 1990). Black-box assumptions and the "psychology of the stranger" work hand in had with the growing division between social classes in society. Methodologies should not be chosen as a way of distancing oneself from other groups or showing how different these "others" are from "us." This is especially true as these marginalized groups are included in society by social policies.

Although cost-benefit analyses and experimental design will always have a place in policy research, we have come to a point when they are simply not enough to grasp the change process in those individuals whose behavior we want to modify. Our reliance over the last three decades on program evaluations and environmental assumptions about human nature have led to a kind of research that overestimates the importance of formal program goals and the ability of implementers to achieve them. This style of research underestimates the differences between people and how factors outside the intervention shape how much we do and do not change. If our policy-making is to be based on holding people accountable for what they do, then it might behoove policy makers to understand how the people we want to change think about what they do. Policy analysis should, therefore, move toward research designs that put the person back at the center of inquiry and make him or her less of a stranger to policy makers. This is particularly important when the policy in question leaves a person to fend for herself. As we will see in the discussion to come, this is precisely what welfare reform did.

People can be stubborn, selfless, self-defeating, innovative, and adaptable. Their outlook and disposition are shaped by their experiences, their interpretations, and their identities. Therefore, maybe the differences in program outcomes arise because *individuals* are reacting to interventions. Maybe people behave in a way that is consistent with their "story" of who they are, rather than simply as rational calculators. The person's sense of self and her strengths will determine how she does in this market-driven environment, and those with fewer natural resources will continue to fare poorly while those with more resources will fare better. The latter group will be limited by the structures of race, class, and gender, which still shape life chances in America. Welfare reform sets individuals adrift or free (depending on your perspective). We need to know those persons better.

If this approach makes sense, then we need to look at both how people reacted to the new welfare law and how those reactions differed among the people affected by the reform. We also need to map those reactions in the context of the liberal and conservative predictions as to the impact of the reform. We have argued that neither perspective captures the reality of the situation for the poor, but saying that and showing it are two very different things. In the next chapter we will outline the liberal and conservative perspectives on welfare reform, analyzing the thought of the leading intellectual proponents of each perspective. We will then contrast the predictions each perspective would have for welfare reform. These contrasts will frame our analysis as we describe how welfare reform affected the poor in Illinois. We will describe how the conservative analysis of welfare reform predicted that as recipients were forced off the rolls and were required to work, their lives would take on a more positive direction. Work would mean more income and that would bode well for their mental health and the prospects of their children. More income would mean living in a better community and having prospects for a brighter future. In the liberal analysis, the trajectory was seen as down and negative. Being forced off welfare would mean less income and little prospect for meaningful work. This lack of resources would spell trouble for the children in the family. Families with less income would be forced into bad neighborhoods. The contrast between the conservative and liberal analyses could not be more stark. We will see how the lives of the poor comport to the predictions the contending perspectives offered.

The book unfolds as follows. In the next chapter, we examine the Illinois political culture in more depth and its impact on the final set of welfare policies developed in response to the 1996 federal initiative. We will show that political culture really matters when it comes to explaining the approaches different states took to meeting the requirements of PRWORA. We will show how that political culture produced a set of policies that led to some very positive outcomes. Chapter 3 describes the Illinois Families Study, the main source of data and information for this book. The sample of over one thousand women who were on welfare when the reform was implemented and whom we followed for four years provides the foundation for the research we report. Chapter 4 provides an overview of welfare caseload trends in Illinois since 1996. Chapters 5 through 10 detail how Illinois families are faring, based on in-depth interviews with a set of families in the Illinois Families Study between 1996 and 2000. The data show some encouraging as well as disturbing findings. While many have left welfare, not all have left for jobs. In fact, a large percentage are neither working nor receiving welfare, which raises the question of how they are surviving. Those who are working are earning low wages, and many are living just barely above the poverty line. Those still on welfare are some of the most vulnerable families in the state, and with a welfare clock ticking, their futures are worrisome. In Chapter 5, I look more closely at work and earnings, determining which personal factors place people at an advantage in the work world, and which impede progress. Not surprisingly, we find that human capital (education, job skills) and personal motivation separate workers from nonworkers. In this post-welfare world, it is personal characteristics that will make or break one's future. Many have argued that the welfare program is a needed safety net for those facing sizable barriers to work and self-sufficiency. In Chapter 6, I look at one of those barriers—depression—in depth. Chapter 7 describes how the children fare in school. Chapter 8 examines the effects in Illinois of its sanction policy—whether sanctions are indeed the needed spur for families to leave welfare for work, or whether, in contrast, sanctions are hurting those most in need of the support. Chapter 9 looks beyond the women themselves to their children, examining how children of welfare recipients are faring in school and whether problematic behavior is improving or regressing. I conclude with a review of our results that I contrast with the liberal and conservative approaches and suggest what we have learned by applying a person-centered approach to welfare reform.

A word or two about the data presented in the chapters to come. The primary source of data in this book is the Illinois Families Study (IFS). This panel survey interviewed the same 1,300 women who had been on welfare in Illinois when the federal reform went into effect. They were interviewed annually for four years. Additionally, annual qualitative in-depth interviews were conducted with a subsample of this group for two years. Administrative data were matched to those of the entire sample, giving us data on Medicaid and Food Stamp enrollment and wage data through the Unemployment Insurance information available through the state. While we employ different data analysis techniques, the information presented in the coming chapters is all taken from these two data sets. The number of the different subsamples employed for these analyses changes for a variety of reasons (missing data being the most common one), but it is all based on the same random sample of recipients who were tracked and interviewed over the four years of the study.

CHAPTER 2

Making the Words Flesh

Welfare Reform in the Illinois Political Culture

IN 1996 THE FEDERAL GOVERNMENT radically reformed the country's welfare system, the centerpiece of which was the cash assistance program Aid to Families with Dependent Children (AFDC). The AFDC program, first introduced more than fifty years ago, offered cash assistance to mothers who had been abandoned or widowed to help make ends meet and support their children without having to work. Several factors that converged in the latter half of the twentieth century, however—including a rise in single motherhood and the persistence of poverty—cast a pall over the cash assistance program. By the early 1990s, in the eyes of reform advocates and most of the public, AFDC consigned poor mothers to a world of dependency and pathology, or at the very least continued poverty. Advocates of reform looked at AFDC and theorized that dependency created by the welfare system trapped people and kept them poor (Murray, 1984; Mead, 1986; Ellwood, 1988), mainly by discouraging them from working.

Scholars vigorously debated whether welfare discouraged work and led to continued poverty. For nearly every study that held up evidence of a perverse incentive created by welfare, there was a counter-study showing that welfare was a safety net, used on average only for a few years while a woman got on her feet again. Although certainly convincing from a research standpoint, these latter studies did not win out in the minds of the public, who instead were swayed by images of "welfare queens" and felt strongly that taking cash "handouts" was not the American way.

As the numbers on welfare remained high even as the economy began to improve in the late 1980s, and as more children were born into single-mother households, politicians began to clamor for answers to this problem of welfare. Clearly, there had been major changes in both those who used welfare and the public's support of the program. When Aid to Dependent Children (later Aid to Families with Dependent Children) was begun in the 1930s, it was intended to support widowed mothers, but by 1973 it was increasingly supporting African American single mothers among its eleven million beneficiaries. Attempts by Kennedy, Johnson, Nixon, Carter, and Reagan to reform the system met with defeat. While most efforts attempted to tie work to welfare, the stagnant economy of the 1970s and early 1980s left too many with too few job options. The polarizing stances between liberals and conservatives on the causes of poverty further entrenched the political parties, ensuring little would be done to reform welfare.

By the beginning of the 1990s, answers to poverty and welfare seemed even more elusive. A crack-cocaine epidemic was beginning to ravage the nation's inner cities (home to a sizable welfare population), children were flooding child-welfare agencies, homicide rates among young black men were soaring, and poverty and single motherhood seemed a way of life for too many of the nation's minority children. Nearly one-half of African American children in 1993 were living in poverty, compared with roughly 10 percent of white children (Nichols, 2006). The public was tired, impatient—and far removed from the realities of life on the ground for the inner-city poor.

Onto the scene came a charismatic man with a personal story of near-poverty himself, President Bill Clinton. Making it his mission to "end welfare as we know it," he formed a bipartisan committee to reform welfare, while at the same time the Republican-controlled House of Representatives worked on its own legislation under the "Contract with America" movement. Both Clinton and the House drew inspiration from states' experiments with state-based welfare policies. These experiments had been going on for several years under waivers from federal rules. States had been experimenting with financial incentives, incentives to limit the number of children in welfare families, eligibility rules, and other measures. Perhaps the most fundamental change, however, was found in a handful of states that imposed a time limit on welfare reform. Under AFDC, welfare had been a hard-fought entitlement. Individuals were entitled to cash support for as long as they were eligible—in other words, for as long as they were poor. The time limit and work mandates would come to symbolize the conservative shift towards welfare reform. By the end of the 1980s, two distinct approaches to welfare reform had emerged. The liberal and conservative approaches to welfare reform are reflected in the work of two scholars, Charles Murray, representing the conservative approach, and David Ellwood, representing the liberal. We will analyze the seminal works of these two authors to highlight the very different perspectives that battled over how to improve the welfare situation.

Charles Murray and the Conservative Answer

For various reasons, the welfare system was dysfunctional in many people's eyes, articulated perhaps most clearly by Charles Murray in his influential book *Losing Ground* (1984). Murray built his analysis of the welfare problem on how liberal policy shaped the person on welfare. He argued—and conservatives adopted this view—that an intellectual coup by a small group of liberal elites had hijacked domestic federal policy during the 1960s, and that their ideas had won the day. This intelligentsia, Murray said, convinced America to approach social problems by arguing that the "system" was to blame for the situation in which the poor and other disadvantaged groups found themselves. This system was not just the government but also the economic structure, racism, and the arrangement of social institutions, all of which limited the poor's participation in the economy. According to the liberal position that Murray disputed, the individual was no longer responsible for how he or she fared. Because the source of this disadvantage was to be found in economic and social relations, the government's job was to remedy that disadvantage with resources, such as housing assistance, cash assistance, and so forth.

Murray summarized the liberal position in the following way:

> What emerged in the mid-1960s was an almost unbroken intellectual consensus that the individualist explanation of poverty was altogether outmoded and reactionary. Poverty was not a consequence of indolence or vice. It was not the just deserts of people who didn't try hard enough. It was produced by conditions that had nothing to do with individual virtue or effort. Poverty was not the fault of the individual but of the system. (p. 29)

According to Murray, government programs then created a set of rules and regulations that the needy person took advantage of in perfectly rational ways. It was the government program rather than race or culture or individual pathologies that produced the counterproductive behaviors. In his classic discussion of a fictionalized couple, Harold and Phyllis, Murray showed how, under a set of policies that predated the blame-the-system thinking, the couple would marry after discovering that Phyllis was pregnant, and Harold would go to work. Once the blame-the-system approach of the middle 1960s was in place, Phyllis and Harold would have the child and live together without marrying, and Harold would not go to work but instead would live off Phyllis's welfare benefits. Harold and Phyllis are acting rationally given the options provided.

The Liberal Response—*David Ellwood*

The closest the liberals came to a counteroffensive to the conservative argument was in David Ellwood's now classic book *Poor Support* (1988). To address poverty, he argues, we must acknowledge the link between values and outcomes; failing to uphold our values can result in negative outcomes, such as poverty. Ellwood argues that liberals and conservatives could find common ground by recognizing common values, including autonomy of the individual, the virtue of work, the primacy of the family, and the desire for a sense of community. From these tenets flow individual beliefs about behavior and expectations for others. The key to a healthy polity, he argues, is to create policy consistent with values. When policy is consistent with values, it is the solution and never the cause of the problem. Without such consistency, negative consequences result. Here Ellwood turns to the classic liberal value of knowledge as a means to progress. It is only in first knowing the causes of poverty, he argues, that we can then propose solutions that are consistent with our shared values.

Problematically, however, Ellwood, unlike Murray, does not address the way in which individual behavior serves as a link between values and poverty, nor does he offer an explanation for how behaviors, or choices, are shaped. Rather, he assumes that individuals will always act in accordance with their values, and that those individuals are essentially good. He writes:

> The best hope is to understand the real causes of poverty and to address them directly. The goal ought to be to ensure that everyone who behaves responsibly will avoid poverty and welfare. The big challenges to be tackled involve supporting the working poor, resolving the dual role of single parents, helping people over temporary difficulties, and offering hope to all people that they can get a job if they are willing to work. (p. 237)

In other words, he sets forth the agreed-on values that should guide poverty policy, but he assumes his new policies will shape behavior, even though the old policies did not. At the end of his analysis, competing values are still in tension. His proposals can be seen as attempts to address the outcomes rather than the causes of poverty. On the surface, his suggestions for reform, which include ensuring medical protection, increasing the earnings of working families, enforcing child support, making assistance temporary, and creating jobs for the unemployed, seem to offer a new understanding of poverty and welfare. And although they do address some of the inconsistencies in the older entitlement system, they still subscribe to a notion of government in which the role of the policy maker is to react to negative economic consequences. For Ellwood, problems lead to policy. For Murray, policy leads to problems. For the latter, the person is shaped by that policy; for the former, if the person is shaped by the new policy, it is in ways that are left vague and unspecified.

The Conservatives Triumph

What was the result of the liberal versus conservative debate? Murray's logic was far more persuasive. In 1996, Congress passed the Personal

Responsibility and Work Opportunity Reconciliation Act (PRWORA), which for the first time made welfare contingent on work and set lifetime limits on welfare receipt. Now called Temporary Assistance for Needy Families (TANF), cash assistance (formerly AFDC) was, as the name said, temporary and work-based. In essence, the policy marked a shift away from empathy and toward accountability, away from entitlement and toward very limited support. TANF said simply: go to work, the state will no longer support you indefinitely.

The law also expanded states' flexibility to design and manage their own TANF programs. This freedom reflected the larger movement in the federal government to "devolve" planning and fiscal responsibility to the states. Dictating policies from on high that might not fit local cultures, economies, and on-the-ground realities was out of vogue. Instead of designing an overarching federal welfare policy, the federal government laid out some broad parameters (many of which had originated in the states under waiver experiments) within which states could design and manage their own welfare programs. The federal government gave a lump sum of money (known as a block grant in policy circles) to each state to fund and design its TANF and welfare-to-work programs. It also designed incentives for states to cut their welfare rolls. Each state's block grant was funded at its 1992–1995 spending levels. If they spent less, states could keep the money for future years or divert it to other related programs, such as child care. But if states failed to move an increasing proportion of their welfare caseload into the workforce each year, they faced fiscal penalties.

Welfare Reform in the States—*Illinois as an Example*

The debate over welfare reform was being conducted in state houses throughout the early 1990s. The passage of the Family Support Act in 1987 had triggered legislation in many states to change how welfare was administered. The waivers to federal rules granted throughout the early 1990s tasked state legislators to think through how they wanted to change policies. Democrats and Republicans worked to define new ways to deliver welfare programs at the state level. Nineteen ninety-four was a pivotal year, as the Republicans won majorities in many state houses.

Illinois, the focus of this book, was among those states both revising their welfare programs and ushering in a Republican administration. As Mead (2006) and others have suggested, state political cultures shaped the nature of the reforms introduced both before and after the 1996 federal legislation. Illinois's policy reflected the political culture of the state—one of Midwestern pragmatism minus the history of socialist workers' rights radicalism of other Midwestern states such as Minnesota and Wisconsin. Illinois has been described as having an "individualist political culture" (Elazar, 1984) that emphasizes the democratic order of the marketplace.

Government's purpose is utilitarian, merely managing the popular demands for services and maintaining an open competitive market. The market, this stance would argue, does and should organize society, dictating what the government can and should do, and in this sense the market sets the limits of what is possible for state government. The result is a modest state political agenda that keeps taxes low and does not undertake major redistributive efforts. Government intervention is minimal, and regulations are conducive to the growth of business.

The Democratic and Republican parties, although competitive, were not, in the late 1980s and early 1990s, distinguished by major ideological differences. Rather, the parties represented regions of the state, and the statewide contests centered on which party better represented centrist values. The design of TANF in Illinois reflects the individualist culture of the state. A welfare policy consistent with the state's culture should be assessed in terms of how it shapes the recipients' work effort and family organization, and on the tax demands it imposes on the business community. If welfare weakens workers' ties to the labor market and shrinks the pool of available workers, it must be reformed. Welfare reforms should therefore serve the market in more rational and efficient ways.

Following this logic, welfare reform in Illinois has had three basic objectives: to curb the rolls, keep costs under control, and produce more income and opportunity for previously eligible welfare families. Like most states, Illinois is reluctant to spend state tax dollars on welfare. Most states limit welfare spending to programs to get people off welfare in parallel with strict attempts to limit costs generally. These efforts are couched in talk of getting people back to work and training them for the labor market. The trick after PRWORA was to link less welfare participation with more—or at least not less—opportunity.

The Illinois General Assembly completed the state's TANF plan in early 1997, and the changes were implemented in July of that year. With Republicans winning both the state House and Senate in 1994, and Newt Gingrich and his fellow Republicans sweeping the U.S. House of Representatives, welfare reform wasn't a surprising development. Following the TANF victory and with a Republican governor in office, Illinois put in place a "work first" strategy that promoted work experience over education or training as the key to advancement. TANF recipients with children older than thirteen were required to work eighty hours a month or lose benefits. PRWORA in 1997 imposed a total of five years' lifetime limit on cash assistance.

Those who failed to follow the welfare rules were sanctioned in a series of increasingly punitive measures. The state also created a set of work-related supports, including child-care subsidies, continued health insurance under Medicaid, and the Earned Income Tax Credit, a tax break for low-income workers (although Illinois has one of the lowest state EITCs in the country).

One of the more unusual, and important, features of the Illinois plan, and one also reflecting the culture of state policy-making, was the "stopped clock" provision. This allowed a welfare recipient to stop the clock on the five-year countdown if she met one of the following conditions: (1) was working at least 30 hours a week, (2) was participating full-time in a postsecondary degree program and maintaining a minimum grade point average of 2.5, (3) was responsible for a medically dependent child or a disabled spouse, or (4) had received a domestic violence exclusion.

The Work Pays income disregard was another important part of the reform. It allowed workers to keep $2 of every $3 earned, rather than losing $1 in benefits for every $1 earned, as they had under AFDC. Considered a needed work incentive by policy makers and others, this "earnings disregard" had been instituted in 1993, a year before the Republican administration took over. The system also sought to curb a perceived fault of the former system, the incentive to have more children in order to receive higher welfare payments. A "family cap" was imposed under which any additional children born to welfare recipients after January 2004 would not bring in higher benefits. State culture and federal reforms were in perfect harmony in these policies, which reflected the state tradition of supporting labor markets and limiting state responsibility for the poor. The commitment was to strengthen competitive markets while keeping taxes low.

The national scene also reflected a major transformation in welfare policy. Given the backdrop of accountability, time limits, mandated work, and an end to blame-the-system liberal thinking, how have families fared ten-plus years after welfare reform? On the surface, the effect was immediate. Within a few years, welfare caseloads nationally were cut in half. More single mothers (and women in general) are working today, although poverty rates have not improved significantly. Poverty in the initial years after welfare reform dropped significantly, and many claimed that welfare reform was the reason. However, the economy in the late 1990s was booming, and entry-level jobs were plentiful. In addition, the federal government greatly expanded the Earned Income Tax Credit. The tax credit for low-income workers has since been called the nation's most effective antipoverty program, responsible for lifting four million families out of poverty. At its maximum, certain working families can receive $4,400 a year from the credit (refunds are based on earnings and family size). Since the economic downturn of the early 2000s, the poverty rate crept back up and was at 12.6 percent in 2005. Nevertheless, it is still lower than in 1996, when 13.7 percent of the nation's population was living in poverty.

"Personal responsibility"—no more blaming the system, accountability, time limits, work mandates—Murray's argument in action. In this world, where all responsibility is individual (with the state essentially washing its hands of the problem after five years), one could surmise that the fittest will survive and thrive (and probably benefit the most from a policy that essentially gives them needed incentives to leave welfare). If welfare is temporary and requires work, most recipients will see the need to leave quickly. Those persons with strengths and skills will have a better chance at success. But what about the rest—those with barriers to work (mental health limitations, lack of job experience, lack of education, and so forth)? In a work-first system, these might not fare as well.

We offer some insights on this issue after tracking a large group of Illinois welfare recipients for five years, documenting their personal well-being, and identifying how the new policies are affecting families in Illinois. Illinois welfare recipients are an excellent case study because in many ways they are representative of national welfare caseloads. Illinois had, in 1996, the fourth largest welfare caseload in the nation. The state is also home to Chicago, a large city with many of the classic challenges of inner-city America, as well as several midsized cities. It also has a large rural population, which is often overlooked in welfare studies. Rural poverty is actually higher and more persistent than urban poverty. Finally, in 1996, unemployment in the state was on par with the national average.

Illinois's individualistic political culture emphasizes the democratic order of the marketplace, with the government's role as strictly utilitarian: to handle the functions demanded by the people it serves. This culture, as we have already suggested, defined the welfare "problem" in the early 1990s—a problem that was becoming increasingly apparent as poverty and welfare rolls in Illinois climbed in the 1970s and 1980s—in a nonpartisan way. The poverty rate in Illinois rose from 10.2 percent to 15.3 percent between 1969 and 1992, a 50 percent increase in little more than twenty years. Other Midwestern states also experienced rising poverty rates during this period, but the increase in Illinois was greater than in these states and greater than in the nation as a whole. Illinois did fare somewhat better during the economic downturn of the early 1980s when other states—Indiana, Iowa, and Michigan, for example— experienced larger increases in poverty. Figure 2.1 shows the poverty rates in the six years prior to welfare reform in 1996. By 1994, the Illinois poverty rate, at 12.4 percent, had dipped from its high of 15.3 percent in 1992, while that of other states (notably Indiana, Michigan, and Ohio) was still increasing.

With rising poverty came rising rates of welfare use. The monthly average in the number of persons receiving AFDC in Illinois fluctuated during the 1980s, ending the decade at 632,000, but there would be a steady increase through 1996 (see figure 2.2).[1] These rising caseloads were a major impetus for reform.

Unemployment also fluctuated between 1981 and 1993, and, not surprisingly, peaks in AFDC followed shortly after peaks in unemployment. The Illinois unemployment rate was consistently higher than the rate nationally and in most Midwestern states except Michigan and Ohio.

FIGURE 2.1—Poverty Rates in Midwestern States Prior to Welfare Reform

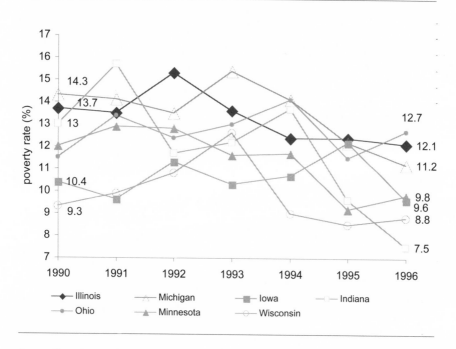

Source: Committee on Ways and Means, 199X Green Book.

The birth rates of teenage mothers and of single-parent families rose in Illinois as well as nationally. Between 1982 and 1991, the national birth rates for 15- to 19-year-old women of all races rose from 52.4 per 1000 to 61.8 per 1000 (U.S. Department of Health and Human Services, various years). The teen birth rate was lower for white women but was also on the rise, from 41.2 in 1982 to 43.3 in 1991. Black women had the highest teen birth rates as well as the greatest increase in birth rates over time. The 1980 teen birth rate for black women was 97.8, increasing to 115.5 by 1991. In Illinois, the birth rate per 1000 females aged 15 to 19 was significantly higher than the national rate, which was 62.9 in 1990, and the rate had been rising slowly since 1985. The teen birth rate among non-Hispanic whites in 1990 was lower than national rates, at 36.5, but rates for black teens were higher than national figures, at 146.2. By 2002, this rate would decline to 22.3 for non-Hispanic whites and 82.6 for non-Hispanic blacks.

An increase in birth rates occurred during the 1980s not just among teens but also among all unmarried women. In 1991, 38 percent of all first births in Illinois were to unmarried women, including 83 percent of

FIGURE 2.2—Total AFDC Recipients in Midwestern States, Selected Fiscal Years, 1965–1996

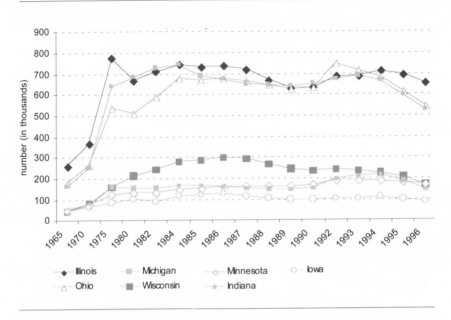

Source: U.S. Dept of Health and Human Services, AFDC: *The Baseline*, June 1998. Available at http://aspe.hhs.gov/HSP/AFDC/afdcbase98exhib.htm#list

African American births, 45 percent of Hispanic births, and 23 percent of white births (American Enterprise Institute, 1994). Also in 1991, 22 percent of all first-born children went on welfare. Although the rate of unmarried pregnancy was highest among black women, the rate of increase for unmarried black women was much lower than for whites or all races in Illinois. Between 1985 and 1991, the ratio of births to unmarried women increased 46 percent among white women and 27 percent among women of all races, while the increase for black women was just 8 percent (U.S. Department of Health and Human Services, various years).

With the exception of pockets of white rural poverty in the southern portion of the state, a person in poverty in Illinois is likely to be black. The state has a sizable black population, mainly in the metropolitan Chicago area and in downstate St. Clair County. In 1992 in Illinois, AFDC receipt was highest among the black population (table 2.1). Of all AFDC recipients, 60.7 percent were black, 29 percent were white, 10 percent were Hispanic, and less than 1 percent were Asian. This distribution was much more heavily African American than in other Midwestern states and in the nation as a whole.

TABLE 2.1—Percentage Distribution of AFDC Cases by Race, September 1992

	White	*Black*	*Hispanic*	*Asian*
Illinois	28.9	60.7	9.9	0.5
Indiana	52.8	36.6	2.2	0.1
Iowa	84.6	11.9	1.3	1.0
Michigan	48.9	47.2	2.7	0.4
Minnesota	62.6	18.2	3.1	8.1
Missouri	54.5	44.2	0.7	0.5
Ohio	59.1	38.4	2.1	0.2
Wisconsin	48.7	37.2	6.2	4.4
U.S. Total	38.9	37.2	17.8	2.8

Source: Committee on Ways and Means, U.S. House of Representatives, *1994 Green Book*, pp. 412–413

Public Assistance Benefits Reduced

Although poverty persisted during the 1980s and the early 1990s, public assistance benefits in Illinois deteriorated significantly. The state's AFDC benefit increased only three times, and at $377 in 1995 was only $75 more than it had been in 1982. At the same time, the discrepancy between the actual Illinois AFDC monthly benefit for a family of three and the Illinois state poverty index, or standard of need (an adjustment to the federal poverty level based on state conditions), increased significantly. The standard of need increased annually from $486 in 1982 to $936 in 1995. The AFDC benefit declined from 62 percent of the standard of need in 1982 to only 40 percent of the standard of need in 1995. Among Midwestern states, Illinois in 1994 was below all but Ohio, Indiana, and Missouri in AFDC benefit amounts, and lower than all but Ohio and Missouri in the benefit amount as a proportion of the standard of need (Committee on Ways and Means, U.S. House of Representatives, 1994).

Compared with other Midwestern states, Illinois had the smallest absolute increase in AFDC benefits between 1970 and 1994, as well as the lowest percentage increase (table 2.2). The AFDC benefit in Illinois increased during this period by only 58 percent, while the other Midwestern states had increases of at least 100 percent. Recipients in both Michigan and Wisconsin also experienced a decline in benefits in relation to need, yet they still received higher benefits than those in Illinois.

Public Assistance Expenditures

The cost of AFDC in Illinois remained relatively stable over time compared with other welfare-like programs, such as Supplemental Security Income (SSI), which serves the elderly and disabled nonworkers, and food stamps. Benefits in both the Food Stamp and SSI programs are subject to automatic adjustments for inflation, and SSI also has automatic benefit increases, which partially explains its more consistent rise in expenditure compared with AFDC. In addition, changes in federal eligibility rules increased expenditures in the SSI program. Because AFDC benefits are not subject to automatic increases for inflation, expenditure levels are related more to changes in the unemployment rate and resulting caseloads. Illinois did increase its AFDC benefits in 1981, 1985, and 1990, however, and the increases were offset by declines in the unemployment rate and AFDC caseloads. A comparison with other Midwestern states shows that Illinois was among the least generous in AFDC expenditures over time (table 2.3).

In general, inflation-adjusted overall state spending in Illinois, according to data from the Illinois Department of Public Aid, increased about 17 percent from the early 1980s to 1994. Expenditures in the General Funds, which support education, social services, and the operating and administrative expenses of

TABLE 2.2—Maximum AFDC Benefit in Dollars for a Three-Person Family, Selected Years

	1970	1975	1980	1985	1990	1994	% increase 1970 to 1994
Illinois	232	261	288	341	367	367	58.2
Indiana	120	200	255	256	288	288	140.0
Iowa	201	294	360	360	410	426	111.9
Michigan (Wayne)	219	333	425	468	516	459	109.6
Minnesota	256	330	417	524	532	532	107.8
Missouri	104	120	248	263	289	292	180.8
Ohio	161	204	263	290	334	341	111.8
Wisconsin	184	342	444	533	517	517	181.0
U.S. Total	184	235	288	332	364	366	98.9

Source: Committee on Ways and Means, U.S. House of Representatives, *1994 Green Book*, pp. 375–377

TABLE 2.3—AFDC Benefit Expenditures by State, 1985–1993
($ constant millions)

	Expenditures 1985	*Expenditures 1993*	*Real Change*
Illinois	$869.1	$882.9	-25%
Indiana	153.2	224.8	9
Iowa	159.6	163.3	-24
Michigan	1,197.9	1,190.1	-26
Minnesota	308.3	384	-7
Missouri	195.3	283.8	8
Ohio	759.9	980.5	-4
Wisconsin	556.4	441.2	-41

Source: Committee on Ways and Means, U.S. House of Representatives, *1994 Green Book*, pp. 412–413.

most state agencies, grew from $4.3 million to $5.1 million in inflation-adjusted dollars. Spending on education fluctuated over the twenty years between 1974 and 1994, while spending on Medicaid increased dramatically during the same period and, as we've already seen, spending on AFDC declined.

Welfare's Place in the Political Culture of Illinois

Welfare reform in Illinois has had a handful of core objectives: curb the rolls, keep the costs of welfare under control, and encourage families toward self-sufficiency through work. Instead of spending money on programs designed to get people off the rolls, such as job training and the like, states tend to cut costs. In Illinois prior to welfare reform, moving people from welfare to work was largely a rhetorical device to justify cutting the rolls and reducing costs. It also fit neatly into the free-market philosophy of the state. As Steve Rauschenberger, a Republican leader in the State Senate, said, "In a short period of time you have the added benefit of putting people in the workforce to continue to drive the service needs, while keeping the inflation curve down because in this boom economy [of the late 1990s], we would have run out of employees. I think the welfare reform has more to do with the expansion of the economy than e-commerce and high-tech firms."

Keeping spending levels for human services low and keeping taxes both low and regressive won elections in the decade running up to the 1996 reforms. For many state agencies, spending increases in the 1980s and 1990s were more often the result of class-action suits than of legislative or gubernatorial leadership. These suits led to court-ordered higher spending or consent decrees.

These lawsuits played an important role in the calls for reform. While the most dramatic examples of litigation were in the Illinois Department of Children and Family Services and the Illinois Department of Mental Health and Developmental Disabilities, litigation also played a vital role in the Illinois Department of Public Assistance. For example, a successful court case brought by the Land of Lincoln Legal Assistance Program, a nonprofit group supporting low-income persons, severely curtailed the sanctioning of participants in the Work Incentive (WIN) Demonstration Project, a work-training program of the early 1980s. During the implementation in 1988 of the Family Support Act in Illinois—a program to enforce child support—a lawsuit by the Legal Assistance Foundation in Chicago prevented the state from limiting child-care support to only those mothers formally approved for the Job Opportunities and Basic Skills (JOBS) Program, another welfare-to-work training program. The suit was successful in asserting that the Family Support Act was an entitlement of any AFDC mother who was enrolled in an education, training, or work program.

Such litigation has great political benefit for elected officials operating within the Illinois political culture. Elected officials can say they held the line on taxes—after all, it is the court that is ordering the spending, and one has to obey the law—while at the same time the interest groups and the bureaucracies themselves receive additional funding. Coalitions between Republican officeholders and liberal interest groups shape a politics of reform in the absence, and perhaps to the detriment, of traditional democratic institutions, while producing modest changes in funding patterns. This coalition also places tremendous power in the hands of interest groups, which are not accountable to the public. At the same time, the bureaucracies and the governor can claim with some justification that outside groups have participated in the policy-making process and that the government is responsive to the concerns of liberal reform groups, while in fact it has maintained control of power and the decision-making process.

"No More Welfare"—1995 Illinois Legislation

The Democratic Illinois General Assembly in the early 1990s managed to avoid significant controversy by providing protective support for existing programs. All this changed, however, with the Republican takeover of the General Assembly in 1994. Republicans quickly passed several bills to reform welfare, many of which shared similar provisions with those being discussed nationally. One provision in particular, to eliminate the AFDC program at the end of three years and replace it with an undetermined substitute, revealed the overt hostility to AFDC. Other provisions that passed included:

- A family cap, which barred additional AFDC funds for a child born to a family already receiving welfare.

- Mandated job search for a head of household whose youngest child was age thirteen, unless the head had no high school degree or GED.

- A mandated six-month job search (to the exclusion of education and training activities) for new applicants (or reapplicants) to AFDC who had a high school education or its equivalent or a formal work history and whose youngest child was between ages five and twelve.

  •A two-year time limit on receipt of AFDC for those whose children were age thirteen or older, after which recipients could no longer receive benefits unless they found work.

- The elimination of child-care support unless recipients were working or were in work-related programs for twenty hours or more per week. The only full-time training that would be supported was "short-term."

- Sanctions for persons who volunteered for education and training but became unable to continue their participation. Recipients who were exempted from the JOBS program, typically because their children were under age three, would lose part of their grants if they volunteered for but did not continue in education and training activities.

- Full sanctions (all benefits discontinued) for not reporting earned income.

- A mandated personal plan for employment as a condition of AFDC eligibility.

- A requirement that recipients lacking a high school diploma or equivalent had to be in a work program within two years or would be barred from educational activities.

- Termination of assistance for recipients and children after six months unless paternity was established or the Illinois Department of Public Aid found that the recipients fully cooperated.

- Loss of part of the family's welfare grant if students with poor school attendance did not improve attendance.

In short, at the end of the 1994 legislative session, the message to recipients was that work was paramount and that the state was getting tough on making sure that recipients were making their way toward self-sufficiency. These efforts also reflected the culture of both the state government and the state's residents, especially its business core, which believed in the necessity of work for the health of both the economy and families. Illinois was not alone, of course. As the next few years would reveal, the sentiment was bursting onto the national scene, led by Murray and his conservative brethren in Congress who introduced their "Contract with America."

In Illinois, the Republican majority was short-lived. But even though the Illinois House was returned to Democratic control in 1996, the direction of the welfare program was not affected. The competition between Republicans and Democrats over welfare reform was cast less in ideological than in regional terms. The pro-business, low-tax stance common to both parties meant that welfare options were defined fairly narrowly. New taxes were not on the table, nor were ambitious programs that would lead to financial and political liabilities if federal shares were withdrawn in a weakening economy.

Discussions over the 1995 state reforms and the 1996 federal reforms focused on finding common ground for a pragmatic "work first" strategy that would move more welfare recipients off the rolls and also support work efforts in a low-wage labor market. Republican State Senator David Syverson noted that "there was a growing frustration from the public that many individuals who were capable of working weren't, and the state was letting them slide, letting them get paid for by taxpayer dollars. Complaints from the public, including those on welfare, really fueled the push for reform." Carol Ronen, a Democrat in the House, shared those sentiments, noting that "The impetus for reform came from the belief that too much money was being spent on welfare. The pressure to change was coming from the voting public and also from those on welfare. Revealing the market-based pragmatism of the state, Democrat Ronen saw the impetus for welfare reform as helping to prepare the future workforce. "We need to focus on making sure that people are ready to enter the information- [and] technology-driven world economy. We need to give children the skills that they are going to need to compete in a global economy." Republican representative Caroline Krauss commented to us at the time that "the overwhelming majority of men and women on welfare didn't and don't want to be on welfare, but we didn't provide the necessary support services for them to be able to leave the system. Now we are doing more to help them leave the rolls and enter the workforce."

Republicans still took the lead, capitalizing on the momentum they had established in the 1994 reforms. Tom Johnson, a Republican representative, said, "Republicans led the way. Democrats were caught up in the special interests that got in the way of real reform. These groups were afraid to change the system." Republican State Senator Steve Rauschenberger noted, however, that while Republicans led the reform efforts, the lack of change had been less a factor of partisanship than of inertia:

It is difficult to force change on people who have been a long time in the system and are comfortable, albeit not satisfied, with the system as it is. They are not risk takers. But the turnover in the House and Senate [in 1994] led to more people who were willing to take risks and willing to adopt new policies. The reform movement had less to do with the partisanship and more to do with the fact that there were more new legislators in the General Assembly than in most normal years.

Or, as Democratic senator Miguel del Valle said, Democrats expected Republicans to take the lead on an issue that had national momentum and might have done so themselves if they were in control:

The issue of welfare reform was bipartisan in a sense. We knew it was going to be on the national agenda. . . . Then the Republicans took over the [Illinois] House and Senate and put welfare reform on the fast track. They made it a wedge issue. There was a strong push on the part of the Republicans, and this was anticipated and expected by Democrats. It was aggressively led by Republicans. . . . I'm not saying Democrats wouldn't have pushed for welfare reform if we had been in control, but it was a Republican issue.

Democratic representative Lou Lang captured the zeal for reforms. "One of the things they [Republicans] did in a very simple way," he said, "without any research, without looking ahead, was to say in a very simple, one-paragraph bill, no more welfare." By 1997, when TANF was authorized, even the advocacy groups for the poor were on board. Although legislators had passed the welfare reforms with little input from these groups, the deputy director of advocacy at the National Center on Poverty Law, a group that works on behalf of welfare recipients, said that its role as an advocacy group was to "teach everyone about what was in the TANF bill, what other states were doing, and what the bottom lines were. Advocacy groups helped to build a consensus and worked with coalitions."

Lang saw the situation differently. "Advocacy groups played little in the debate because they were ignored. The Republican Party was hell-bent on passing a bill ending welfare. The advocacy groups had no impact because there was nothing to negotiate."

Republicans saw welfare reform differently. "The advocacy groups," said Rauschenberger, "were so comfortable with the system as it was and so comfortable arguing for what they believed the changes ought to be that they weren't willing to do a paradigm shift and step back and say, 'How can we do this better?'"

Republican representative Rosemary Mulligan said that it was in the interests of the state's businesspeople to support job training: "Business really needs to be committed to working with education and job training because these are the employees of the future. We need to make sure business is helping to ensure the success of the new reform measures. The force of how Illinois treats its economy is crucial to making sure that there are jobs for everyone who needs one."

Many Illinois Republicans we interviewed expressed an interest in investing more in job training and education. One commented, "We haven't cut budgets; in fact, we have increased the budget if you consider child care, Medicaid, job training, and education. Illinois has taken the role to provide support, and the emphasis is toward gainful employment, education, and health care." As Rauschenberger explained, welfare wouldn't succeed without attention to other issues:

> Three things need to be addressed and need to be addressed much better for welfare to be a success in the long run. We have to make sure child care is available, we have to stay focused on transportation issues, and we have to deal with the question of medical coverage. If you really want to stabilize these people, and I think we do because we have a social interest and a humanitarian interest, we have to keep those interests in mind if we really want to improve.

Conclusion

Given the flexibility provided by the 1996 federal law, Illinois lawmakers were able to craft a response that reflected the state's individualistic political culture. That culture solved problems in a utilitarian way, spending to facilitate the poor person's entrance into the labor market with the resources needed to "make work pay." The Illinois law was not punitive, but it did force welfare recipients into work. The law did provide some of the tools (child care, health insurance, food stamps, earned income disregard, etc.) necessary to living at or near the minimum wage. In many ways, if national welfare reform was to work, Illinois was a good test case. Illinois lawmakers were ahead of the curve in anticipating the federal reform, and both political parties took to heart the charge of lowering the welfare rolls and giving former recipients some of the tools they would need to care for their children and support themselves in the labor market. We now turn to how welfare recipients did in this new world beyond AFDC.

CHAPTER 3

The Illinois Families Study

WITH PASSAGE OF THE FEDERAL PERSONAL Responsibility and Work Opportunity Reconciliation Act in August 1996, Illinois followed federal requirements and implemented its own reforms in July 1997, coupling its experience with various waiver programs it had been piloting with the mandates of the new TANF laws. As we discussed in the previous chapter, the political culture of the state led to a supportive but pragmatic interpretation of the federal law. Illinois's TANF program extended and expanded an earned income disregard to 66.7 percent—meaning that for every $3 earned while on TANF, a recipient could keep $2, rather than the dollar-for-dollar reduction under the old AFDC program. It also instituted a sixty-month lifetime limit on receipt of cash assistance, although months when the recipient was working at least thirty hours a week weren't counted toward the limit. This "stopped clock" option was more generous than that of several neighboring states. Illinois also instituted a family cap, whereby additional children born to a welfare recipient did not increase the size of the cash grant. The state also instituted a series of sanctions for not following the new rules.

Illinois was far from being as draconian as some states (mostly in the South), but less liberal than others (for example, California and New York). Connecticut, for example, implemented a more generous financial incentive for working by exempting 100 percent of earnings up to the federal poverty line. Maryland, in contrast, disregarded only 20 percent of earned income. California adopted a "work first" policy that argued, based on pre-reform experiments (Freedman, Friedlander, & Riccio, 1993), that training and education were less effective in raising earnings than was job experience.

When Congress passed PRWORA, it also promoted continued rigorous evaluations of the policies. Illinois followed this lead and instituted several ongoing studies of various aspects of reform. Following passage in Illinois of the Welfare Reform Research and Accountability Act (P.A. 90–74), the director of the Illinois Department of Human Services appointed me, and, with a group of professors from four other Illinois universities, I implemented a five-year panel study of reform in Illinois, called the Illinois Families Study (IFS). The IFS data are the basis for this book. The primary goal of the IFS was to produce annual reports for the legislature to monitor the progress of reforms (or lack of progress) designed to move people off the welfare rolls and into the workforce.

The Illinois Families Study (IFS) began in 1998, when welfare reform was just getting under way, and followed the progress of about one thousand randomly selected welfare recipients for five years, surveying them annually from 1999 through 2003.[1] In addition to documenting trends in their well-being, their workforce participation, their earnings, and many other facets of their lives, we conducted in-depth interviews with about sixty randomly selected women annually throughout the study, and through those interviews we gained considerable insight into their situations and struggles.[2]

The response rates for the IFS study—an important indicator of reliability in any study—were 72 percent in wave 1 (1999), or 1,363 individuals; 87 percent for wave 2 (1,183 respondents); 91 percent for wave 3 (1,072); and 91 percent for wave 4 in 2003 (967).[3] The majority of the analysis in this book relies on the 967 women remaining in the final wave of the study. Statistical adjustments were made in an attempt to make their responses reflect what the full original random sample would have reported. It is important to mention that the participants were chosen by random selection, which ensures that the respondents were not unique in ways that might influence outcomes. For example, if one were to use participants in only a welfare-to-work sample, the results might be biased because people seeking such a program may have more motivation or work-related skills.

Random sampling creates a picture over time of the wide range of persons who are on welfare at any given point. By tracking them prospectively, we can chart the ups and downs of their complex experiences. Finally, to eliminate the risk of under- or overreporting, we do not rely on women's own reports of income, earnings, and labor force participation. Rather, we measure these with Illinois state Unemployment Insurance records, which contain information on employment status and earnings. We also have Medicaid and other administrative records matched to our sample.

The majority of the women are African Americans (85%), but the sample also includes sizable groups of Latinos (13%) and whites (13%). (There is some potential overlap between whites and Hispanics, who may identify as both.) Most of the women in the IFS study live in Cook County, which is home to Chicago and many of its suburbs, especially the inner ring of suburbs. Rural areas of the state are also represented, however, as are some smaller cities. The respondents are in their 20s and 30s (mean age 31.6) and have an average of two to three children. The majority (92%) are single mothers and have relied on welfare for about five years on average. Some live alone with their children, but others live in extended family households. table 3.1 shows the characteristics of the 967 women as measured in the first survey of 1999–2000.

The women support their families with a combination of work, government benefits, odd jobs (such as babysitting, doing nails, braiding hair), child support, and family help. Approximately 15 percent receive child support and another one-third receive informal support from the fathers of their children. The women are eligible for continuing Medicaid and food stamps, even during a short period after they enter the workforce. In our study, by 2003 (two years after the first five-year time limit had kicked in), only 5 percent were receiving the traditional welfare package of TANF, Medicaid, and food stamps, but about one-third still received Medicaid and food stamps without TANF (reflecting the generous work supports the state offered). Nearly one-half were on their own, receiving no benefits from the state. Of the roughly 30 percent who received housing subsidies in 2001, half lived in publicP housing and half held housing vouchers, which can be used to supplement market rents.

Before we detail the various outcomes of welfare reform in Illinois in the next chapter, we first offer a snapshot of three types of recipients in our study. These snapshots are composites compiled to help the reader understand the types of people affected by the reform. While the categories we describe below—which we call "Nurturers," "Strivers," and "the Disaffected"—are composites, real stories from fifty-eight interviewees (their names were changed to protect their identities) are used to exemplify the categories. These conversations helped us form the categories we ultimately identified.

We do not intend to use these composites for anything more than simply setting the stage for a discussion of the ramifications of a policy that blames the individual rather than the system. When you don't fault the system, you are left with personal, individual accountability—personal characteristics will make or break one's success in the work world. Understanding these personal profiles, we argue, is imperative to designing future policies that will support the poor in a post–welfare reform world. Much of the earlier qualitative work on welfare recipients was framed within the liberal paradigm (for example, Edin & Lein, 1997; Duncan, Huston, & Weisner, 2007). The results are profiles that treat respondents as rational actors reacting to overwhelming choices in a reasonable way. Differences between types of people are left, for the most part, unexplored. The assumption is that given the choices poor women have to make, we would all respond similarly. Personalities, traits, and coping styles are left unexamined. Our approach was to look for how these person-level factors affected behavior

TABLE 3.1—Demographic Characteristics of Respondents at Baseline in 1999–2000

	All *(967 respondents)*	*Cook County* *(Chicago metro area)* *(874 respondents)*	*Rest of State* *(93 respondents)*
Mean age	31.6	31.8	30.3
Female	97%	97%	99%
Mean number of children	2.5	2.5	2.5
Mean age of children			
Youngest child	5.2	5.2	5.6
Oldest child	9.6	9.6	9.7
All children	7.4	7.4	7.7
Gave birth as teen	63%	62%	67%
Never married	63%	65%	41%
Divorced	13%	13%	16%
Separated	15%	14%	30%
Married	8%	7%	12%
Widowed	1%	1%	1%
High school graduate or GED	59%	58%	69%
African American	85%	87%	69%
White	13%	11%	31%
Hispanic/Latino	13%	14%	1%
Other	2%	2%	1%

and to put those differences at the center of our analysis. With almost everyone leaving welfare in response to the reforms, this person-centered focus makes more sense, as welfare policy leaves most people on their own, where person-centered factors are going to become more important. The sample for this qualitative study was randomly drawn from a sample of 750 welfare recipients living in the city of Chicago. The initial selection included 150 individuals who were contacted by letter and then by telephone or personally to participate in the study. Sixty-nine agreed to be interviewed in the summer of 2000 (corresponding to a response rate of 46%) and this number was reduced to 58 in 2001 (corresponding to a response rate of 39% of the initial drawing). The current study uses these fifty-seven respondents (we dropped the one male in the qualitative sample for the purposes of this analysis) for whom we had information for both waves of interviews.

Despite the low response rates, t tests comparing the citywide sample (see Appendix B) with the qualitative one reveal no significant differences in several domains considered: age, education, ethnicity, work, work experience, and welfare status. The only significant difference between the two comes from the fact that the citywide sample includes more men than the qualitative study. Aside from this difference, the sample for the qualitative study is representative of the welfare population living in Chicago. (See Appendix B, table B.1 for the sample composition of this study.)

In a total of fifty-eight interviews, all but one of the respondents are female (98%) and the great majority is African American (about 85% of the sample), even though other ethnicities appear in the sample as well: whites (10%), Hispanics or Latinos (3%), and one Native American (2%). The age range of this sample, starting with 18 years old, is rather broad, with most individuals falling into the groups of 20 to 30 years old (41%) and 31 to 40 years old (35%). In terms of education, the sample is equally divided around twelve years of school: 50 percent of respondents have twelve or more years of school while the other 50 percent have less than twelve years. The number of children is also variable, between one and seven, and most respondents have either one (30%) or two (36%) children. Table 3.1 indicates that the majority of individuals in our sample are currently employed (67% work). A minority is still receiving public assistance in the form of welfare benefits (17% of the sample), food stamps, and Medicaid (64% of the sample).

Analysis

Each transcript of the fifty-eight interviews was coded twice, independently, and then content was analyzed by two different researchers. The analysis started with four categories, according to the respondents' status on welfare and work: on welfare/on work; on welfare/off work; off welfare/on work; and off welfare/off work. The content analysis soon made these categories merge with one another and dissolve to a lesser plane, as themes began emerging and demanding a new categorization based on the following domains: children, sources of social support, social relationships, and life difficulties.

The fact that two waves of information on the same person are available in two different periods of time (summer of 2000 and summer of 2001) renders this analysis particularly rich by making accessible not only attitudes and intentions but actual behaviors—which, functioning as a kind of triangulation, added to the reliability of the results.

We divided our sample into three main categories of welfare recipients based on how individuals discussed work and family: Nurturers, Providers, and Disaffected. Providers structure their lives, to a greater or lesser degree, around employment. We identify two main types of Providers: 1) Strivers, composed of the steady ladder climbers and the intermittent career seekers, and 2) Reluctant Providers, who work for mere necessity. Nurturers place their children and family relationships first. The Disaffected appear generally overwhelmed by both family issues and work demands. We reviewed all responses by those interviewed and placed everyone in one of three categories. (See Appendix B, table 2 for a depiction of the three identities we found on a number of policy variables.)

Providers constitute by far the largest group of individuals (71%), while the Disaffected represent only 10 percent of the sample. Providers all work or are involved in school full-time in the pursuit of education for career development purposes. In sharp contrast with this group, Nurturers do not participate in the official workforce, and only 29 percent of the Disaffected are employed. Members of all groups are still receiving cash benefits, although less among Providers than among the other two types. All groups also receive food stamps and Medicaid, alone or in combination, but the group with most members receiving these benefits is the Nurturers.

The average age is the same (31 years old) for the Providers (Strivers and Reluctant), the Nurturers being older (34 years old) and the Disaffected considerably older (39 years old). The level of education does not differ much from group to group, Nurturers being on average the most well educated (13 years of school) and Reluctants the least schooled (an average of 11 years). The average number of children is also about the same for all groups, although a little bigger for Reluctants, who average three.

Nurturers

The first type of welfare recipient is what we label "Nurturers." Nurturers embrace the workforce only reluctantly at best. They would prefer to remain home with their children. As the new welfare law has ratcheted up demands, welfare is more hassle than it is worth in their eyes. This group is more likely to leave welfare, and yet they are also unlikely to find a job. Therefore, they often occupy the no work/no welfare category. They have dropped out of the welfare system, often because of the required job search, the mandatory reporting, and the other stipulations that now come with a welfare check. Their response affects the outcomes that the policy makers see: on the surface, the welfare rolls decline, which is good news. A closer look reveals, however, that a segment of the former recipients have not committed to the labor market. Further, if they are working, they are working in low-paying and part-time jobs, they quit these jobs often, and they put motherhood responsibilities before maintaining their jobs.

One reason for the reluctance toward work is that their children come first. Nurturers often worry that their children would not receive proper care, or that they would miss out on their children's lives if they worked. As Sheila said, "I sit at work and just worry, Are my kids all right? What's going on?" Sheila was relying on the library for child care after school until she could pick up her children at the end of her shift. "I don't like for my children to come to this library because all kinds of things happen there. Besides drug dealing, gang recruitment, pedophiles, and occasional violence, a young white woman comes there to get her fix. On one occasion I found the woman passed out in the stall after an overdose. . . . She still comes to the library to do her thing."

Another woman said, "I don't allow my children to stay home alone. I won't leave my kids with anyone but my family. If I get a job, I will have my family watch my kids. . . . I don't trust people outside my family to even have my kids over for the night."

Another quit her job after coming home to find that her child had diaper rash. "My child never had a rash when she was with me," she said.

Another mother chose to babysit for a woman in the upstairs apartment rather than work outside the home because she prefers to be near her son, who has asthma. "I have to give him asthma treatments almost every day. Plus, I have to take him to the doctor every two weeks. . . . I like being able to work inside the home instead of having to take public transportation across town to get to work, like I did last year. I prefer being able to be by my son and daughter all day."

Vanessa worries that her young son is falling into the wrong crowd while she is at work. Her son, Corey, age 8, is

> . . . hanging with these bad boys, stealing little puppies and stuff. The neighbors tell me that he is out on the streets during the day when he is supposed to be at home. I found a cigarette all crumbled up in his pocket one day. It was one of mine. I was so mad I took him to his dad's house. . . . I can't watch them all the time now and I don't know what they're doing. They don't like the fact that I'm gone a lot with work now.

Although Vanessa's oldest daughter is supposed to care for the children in the evening when Vanessa works, the daughter is unreliable. "I don't like the fact that she only feeds them hot dogs and bread, not real meals. I come home at midnight and they are hungry. They aren't supposed to be up at midnight, let alone hungry."

Nurturers perhaps have always seen work as only a means of putting food on the table. They have not embraced work as a sense of identity or as a route for furthering themselves personally. Dora, for example, grapples with the conflict between her sense of maternal responsibility and her tight financial situation. In the first interview, in 1999, Dora said she was ready to start looking for a job, but she still had not found steady work by the time of the second interview a year later. The last job she'd held was a two-month stint at the post office over the Christmas holiday. Dora's brother and oldest son live with her and help support her. Her brother is epileptic and has developmental disabilities, and Dora is the designated payee for his monthly Social Security check. Her son works at a car wash. Dora reported that she doesn't attend job-training programs because they interfere with her youngest son's schedule, and she does not trust anyone to care for him. According to Dora, all she wants is a job in her neighborhood, but there are none to be found:

> I don't want to work far away while [her youngest son] is still young, because I don't know anyone who could take care of him, and I don't want to leave him with just anyone. I would like to work as a receptionist, or behind a desk as a secretary. I also am qualified to work in a hotel, to do housekeeping, except that I can't lift heavy things. I'm good at reading and writing, and would like to have a clerical job more than anything else. I probably might go back to school or something for some computers, but I can't be concentrating on that right now. I want to do a simple job to make ends meet for me and my baby.

Providers

Compared with Nurturers, Providers have internalized the value of work. Their goal is to leave welfare forever behind. As one mother of two proclaimed, "I'm more motivated, more outspoken. I was a homebody. Now I go out more and am more self-motivated. It's not just the pay but the job that I want." Providers are by far the largest group in our sample, representing more than two-thirds of those we interviewed. For them, welfare reform conformed to their motivations and directions. Not surprisingly, providers were also the most likely to report enjoying their work. "When you are on welfare," says Josephine, "you just want to cry because you can't make ends meet. I try to influence my friends to get up and get a job. I look forward to going to work everyday. You know how kids are at Christmas with toys, well, that's like me going to work every day."

Sabrina revels in her newfound respect from her children. "The way they look at me makes a difference. If they ask for a dollar, I can give it to them."

Providers are often working full-time, making steady incremental gains financially and socially. Proud of their independence, they embrace a career and devise plans to move steadily up the ladder, often by combining additional training and education with their work, and positioning themselves for promotions or better jobs. Rashelle, a single mother with a seven-year-old daughter, exemplifies this ambition and planning. Throughout the year Rashelle works on the weekends as a certified nursing assistant at a nursing home. She also works during the week through a temporary placement agency as a home-care nurse. She is also about to graduate from nursing school with a bachelor of science degree in nursing. Although originally planning to graduate a year earlier, she delayed her graduation because she wanted to be available for her daughter, who was just starting school. "After receiving my BSN degree," Rashelle says, "I hope to get a managerial position at the agency or some other position that will pay more money."

Similarly, Sabrina reported that she has always climbed to a better position or more pay in every job. "At the bus company management reviewed my records and was very impressed. I see someone's technique and then I find a way to do things better than they do." Sabrina volunteers to do tasks that were not in her job description, or she works overtime for no extra pay. "When someone needed something, I knew what to do because I had put in the extra time. I never got a raise for my extra work and wasn't rewarded for my extra effort, but I have the skills that other workers don't. You have to walk in proving yourself so if you're gone, they will know what they are missing."

Strivers are not completely free of welfare; many in fact are still combining work with welfare and other supports. Equal numbers of Strivers and Nurturers interviewed in 1999 had gone to the welfare office to apply in the previous year. Strivers, however, tend to see the system as a lever to catapult them into their futures. This fits right in with the goals of reformers, who envisioned welfare as a temporary and eventually unneeded support. Mary, a Striver, reports, for example, that it was because of welfare that she was able to continue her education. She attended cosmetology school for two and half years. "They [welfare] helped with my uniform, supplies, and bus fare. I never had any complaints. I was fortunate that way. I hear lots of people complaining, not me." Likewise, Mandy, a 30-year-old mother of three, believes she is becoming a more effective parent due to the education and training she has received from state-funded programs. "Welfare helped me get my education and a job as a home health–care provider. I want to be totally off welfare. I'm proud of myself. I went back to school and had one of the top four GPAs in my class. I was the designated person to speak at our graduation."

In July, on a tip from a friend, Mandy applied for and was accepted by a state program that provides training to be a family advocate for pregnant teens. Mandy works full-time during the school year, and over summer vacation she takes classes, paid by the program, that enable her to earn college credits leading to certification as a day-care provider. "I feel that I am improving as a parent, that my job has taught me to raise my children better." Mandy for the first time feels that she is on a professional career track with many opportunities.

Although this group of Providers appears committed to advancing through work, they do not find that the road is always easy. Other responsibilities and realities of life, such as family and children, housing and transportation problems, and a poor economy can become obstacles to their pursuit of work. Despite these hurdles, they tend to be steadily employed and actively try to resolve their difficulties and find new jobs. Part of the difficulty in making ends meet is the low wages most of the women earn, as Maritza reveals:

> It's very difficult. I receive $308 for two weeks of work, and that has to pay taxes, help my mother pay the rent, and cover my kids' expenses. I'm usually left with $50 that has to stretch. The rent here is $500, and this is not a nice neighborhood! . . . What am I going to do? I stretch my money. My kids want stuff, they want to go somewhere, but I can't go. My $50 is for gas. And now I've got a new car, my mother doesn't work anymore. I wish at least they would give me food stamps. I spend $200 in food for the five people living in the house.

Perhaps because of the low wages and limited employment prospects, several Providers are enrolled in higher education, often living on student loans and grants or financial assistance from family members while they finish their education. They typically have well-articulated goals and express realistic expectations for employment after graduation.

In contrast to Nurturers, Providers are better able to maintain a balance between the demands of parenthood and work, devising strategies such as working shifts or relying on extended kin for caregiving. They are also much more comfortable than Nurturers with day-care arrangements, either formal or informal. It is not uncommon among Providers to start work or school by the second or third month after a child's birth and leave the child in the care of family or other day-care providers. Of course, not all arrangements run smoothly, but here again, Providers tend to take it in stride. Tawona, who is employed full-time by a company that sorts bulk mail, has four children who range in age from one to twelve. She says that her children love going to day care, and she is very content with the provider, although "sometimes she puts me in a bind" by taking unexpected vacations. When this happens, Tawona either calls in to work to let them know about the situation or leaves her children with a friend across town. Tawona's boss has little patience for missing work, but her immediate supervisor "really likes me, and she knows that I'm honest. Kids get sick, you know, and I've got four of them."

April, a 42-year-old mother of one, captures the sentiment of many providers, "You know, I'm actually glad the government put a time limit on it (welfare). It made the lazy people go back to work." Perhaps epitomizing the difference between Nurturers and Providers is April's take on paying higher rent. "I think there should be more subsidized housing because paying rent by yourself is hard, so many women struggle." In the past, her subsidized rent had been as low as $139, but now it is $551. However, she laughed and said, "You know I don't mind my rent being so high now because when you think about it, it lets you know you're doing good."

Disaffected

Our final group is "the Disaffected." This group is by far the smallest group of the three, making up only about 10 percent of the entire sample. However, this group is perhaps the most visible, in that the Disaffected fit many of the stereotypes that were bandied about by conservatives in the years leading up to welfare reform. This is the group that is still receiving TANF and not working. Health and emotional problems, combined with low education, long-term dependency, and other personal issues, impede these women from holding, or even considering, steady work. The Disaffected, unlike our other groups, do not define themselves as either mothers or workers. They often describe life as "unfair." Things just happen to them. They appear defeated, demoralized, and lacking in hope or resolve. The prospect of work seems overwhelming to many.

The Disaffected are the most verbal about the wrongs of social institutions, including the welfare system. They tend to blame the system and society for their situation, viewing themselves as victims. "Welfare caseworkers have a terrible attitude," Anita, a mother of four, said. "They are nasty, talk to me like I'm a piece of garbage. I was sanctioned once because my caseworker was reassigned. My new caseworker lost my paperwork, and I was sanctioned even though I handed it all in. Talking to her supervisor didn't help."

Dionne was convinced the caseworker had it out for her:

> This one caseworker just plain didn't like me. She acted like she wanted me to come to the office looking the part of the pauper. I dressed nicely and carried a cell phone. I made the mistake of mentioning that the caseworker could fax something over to me and she got furious over the fact that I had a fax machine. She definitely let me know that I had better act the part of a poor person. Another time when there was a fire in my mother's house, the homeowner's insurance paid for temporary housing until we could return to the house. I called in to the caseworker to tell her about the fire and that I couldn't make the appointment, and the caseworker asked me if I was staying in a homeless shelter. I said no, that we were not at a shelter but were staying at the Hilton. This really got her mad. She said something like, 'What are you doing at the Hilton? You don't belong there,' and she wanted to know exactly who was paying for it. I feel like this was an invasion of my privacy.

The Disaffected are also seemingly nonplussed by the loss of benefits, and their responses reveal perhaps a sense of disconnection from and bewilderment about the system and its demands. Anita, for example, had lost her Medicaid and food stamps four months before the interview. "I don't know the reasons," she said. "I haven't found out why. I think I'll go down there to apply next week." She also reported that her application had been activated for a subsidized housing voucher through Section 8, but that there had been a fire and her papers were destroyed. "I haven't heard from Section 8 about my status. I don't know how or who to talk to." Anita reported that she had been sent by her caseworker to work thirty hours a week in the kitchen of a nursing home. This position lasted for two months and ended when the nursing home closed. Before that she was last employed ten years ago.

The Disaffected also are reluctant to follow the proscriptions of the new system, and many receive financial assistance from family members, most often their parents and often in the form of housing assistance. Thus, as in Wanda's case, dependency can last well into middle age. Unemployed and attending school, Wanda lives with her parents, her four children, her grandmother, and three siblings, all in the same building but on different floors. "I don't know what I'd do [if I weren't with my mother]. I would probably come to a restaurant like this one and stand inside until they hired me. I might ask for old food from restaurants to feed my children. I would make them hire me. I would have to do something." Some also receive child support or support from the men in their lives, although fewer of the Disaffected seem to have the support of the fathers of their children.

Although one might conclude that these women are quick to blame the system and are not holding up their end of the bargain, the stereotypical version of the welfare recipient doesn't address health, mental health problems, domestic violence, and drug abuse. This group was more likely than the employed leavers (that is, those no longer receiving TANF) to report fair or poor health, with primarily mental health issues, including substance abuse and depression.

In addition to physical or mental health problems, several of the women had experienced domestic violence. Dionne, for example, reported that her relationship with the children's father had deteriorated to the point that she had him arrested on abuse charges and sent to jail. She was worried that he would come after her upon his release and regrets that her children witnessed the abuse. Similarly, Wanda's ex-husband had been in prison for a year. Upon his release, "He started doing things to me that I didn't like which he wasn't supposed to do." Wanda's husband also confiscated her paycheck, telling her that she was not allowed to spend her money, even though she argued that her children needed something.

The Disaffected are also deeply troubled by the health of family members, as Valerie, a 46-year-old woman with only a sixth-grade education, described:

I think my daughter is going through that postnatal depression stuff. She is always lying around and crying and walking around in a daze. I'm tired. I can't even think half the time because I'm always thinking about her, worrying about her. I'd like to kick her out because I'm tired of paying for her and caring for her children, but without her, I'll have to pay for child care. My man passed away a couple of weeks ago. I ain't never been this broke or this stressed out. . . . It's been real hard on me. I want to stop talking about him or I'll cry. . . . I'm very alone.

Their own and their families' health problems often have more dramatic implications for the Disaffected than for the other groups, and the health issues seem to last longer. Providers or Nurturers with substance abuse problems tended to have completely recovered at the end of the study. Many of the Disaffected, in contrast, continued to struggle. The same pattern applied to those suffering from depression.

Finally, the Disaffected were nearly twice as likely as our other groups to have doubled up in living arrangements. They were also more likely to have had their utilities cut off, and they were more often worried that they did not have enough money to buy food. They often had no idea how they would survive after reaching their five-year lifetime limit on assistance.

With these profiles in mind, we turn now to some quantitative findings with the full sample from the IFS. We begin with an overview of the effects of welfare reform on Illinois's caseloads in general, and then in subsequent chapters review findings on various factors that influence these outcomes. The findings show how important individual characteristics are in an era of person-centered policies. Who a person is and the internal and external resources she brings to bear on situations become more important in a market-driven environment with limited safety nets. Many previous federal programs were meant to even the playing field for vulnerable populations such as the poor. Without these programs, no matter how flawed they were, individual characteristics matter more. We present a portrait of this new world in the chapters that follow.

SECTION 2

Person-Centered Characteristics

that Influence the Outcomes

of Welfare Reform

Two Worlds of Welfare

Overview of Welfare Caseload Trends in Illinois

MIRRORING NATIONAL TRENDS, welfare caseloads declined sharply in Illinois beginning in the mid-1990s, from a high of 208,646 AFDC cases in 1994 to approximately 25,000 TANF cases in 2003 (the last year of the IFS study) and 33,212 as of 2006. Overall, the Illinois AFDC/TANF caseload declines were more dramatic than those of other upper Midwest states. In fact, the percentage decline was more dramatic than in all but one other state in the nation. Between 1996 and 2003 (the IFS study time span and the years of welfare reform), caseloads in Illinois fell by 85 percent. This compares with a 67 percent decline in Wisconsin (the birthplace of welfare reform), 61 percent in Ohio, 56 percent in Michigan, 54 percent in Minnesota, 50 percent in Iowa, and only 18.5 percent in Indiana (U.S. Dept of Health and Human Services, 2007). These variations by state underscore the importance of state policy and approach, as well as the importance of state economic conditions and other unique conditions in local areas.

An analysis by the Chapin Hall Center for Children at the University of Chicago shows that from 1990 to 1999, a central reason for the dramatic drop in Illinois's welfare caseload was the sharp decline in those entering the system. This was accompanied by less return to welfare and shorter spells on welfare (Lee, Goerge, & Dilts, 2000). Although marked by occasional dips, the number of exits from AFDC/TANF in the state remained fairly stable, while the entries to the program declined significantly beginning in 1997. Our own IFS survey data show that significantly fewer respondents went to a welfare office with the intention of applying for TANF between 1999 and 2003. This suggests that low-income women in the state were getting the message that welfare was no longer a viable option for them.

Emily, a Striver working as a custodian in a nursing home for $6 per hour, appears to have absorbed the new "rules" right in line with reformers' expectations:

> You have to go through so much just to get a little money. I'm going through hell to keep my money. If it was up to me, I would have two or three jobs. They [welfare] don't give you enough, just enough to pay your bills. I think they need to give more to those with children and they should not cut your [food] stamps. . . . I hope that my kids will not be on welfare, and that takes an education and college. By the time my kids grow up there won't be any welfare. They're trying to cut it now, there's going to be a war when there is no more welfare. People have to wait a month now, and they don't like waiting a month. Some don't want a job, but jobs are out there if you want one. You just can't lay around and welfare.

More striking, the proportion of IFS respondents who said their applications were rejected increased. The percentage that applied and received TANF dropped sharply across the four years, to only 39 percent in 2003. With the nation behind welfare reform, and states' funding tied inextricably to their success in lowering caseloads, many TANF offices were diverting applicants with the message that they should apply only if they had exhausted all other options, as Maria, a Striver, reveals:

> Welfare didn't want to help me. I asked them to help me just for one year while I was in school, I said just one year, guys. Please, guys, I have problems with my child. But they didn't help me. So finally I had to quit school. The only good thing about welfare is that it shows you how not to depend on it. Three hundred dollars a month is not enough, so you have to do something about it. That is why I wanted help for six more months, so that I could do something about myself. But I guess that wasn't the way.

Between 1999 and 2003, there was a significant increase in the proportion of IFS respondents who said that someone at the welfare office had told them about the TANF work requirements, but fewer were told to apply for benefits from another program or were given immediate or temporary assistance. Wanda, in our Disaffected group, complains, "There should be emergency assistance available for people needing emergency food or cash. I sold some of my food stamps for cash so I could do laundry and for bus fare. Ten or fifteen years ago, if you applied for welfare and you needed it real bad, they would have given you some emergency help. They don't give it to you now. It'd be three or four weeks before you'd be getting anything, and I'd be starved and died by then."

In the early years of reform, caseworkers were increasingly likely to help applicants devise a plan to support their family without TANF. However, their zealousness subsided by 2003, when the proportions in the IFS sample for whom a plan was devised returned to 1999 levels. This transition, along with less time on welfare, fewer returns after leaving welfare, and many fewer entrants, brought the overall caseload down 85 percent between 1996 and 2006.

The women we interviewed help us to view the caseload decline in more depth. As will become evident, the aggregate caseload decline hides a wide variety of reasons for leaving welfare and a wide variety of views on the position of the welfare system in women's lives. As noted in the prior chapter, Providers, Nurturers, and the Disaffected have very different takes on the system. Nurturers would prefer spending time with their children and would abide by the new rules only reluctantly if at all. The Disaffected are more often bewildered by the changes and have only vague notions of how they will cope once their time limits expire. The Strivers take a completely different approach, as Adrian reveals: "You have to make these programs work for you . . . . I think everyone who needs it should know about everything that's out there to help. This system should make sure that everyone knows what programs are available because knowledge of programs is important and if the caseworker doesn't inform you, you have to find out on your own." Adrian represents many Strivers' views that the system is but a stepping-stone and a temporary support that, if used right, can help them create a new, and better, life. At the same time, she chafes at the intrusion and incompetence: "The thing that aggravates me the most is when you apply for welfare and they ask you to give information about the father, and you give all the information, and to this day they have not given me a child support check, no court date, no nothing. I received a letter from welfare saying that I owe them $791 for overpayment."

Wanda, in the Disaffected category, was less prepared for the change and says "the system doesn't seem fair." Others game the system instead of seeking work, as Irene, a 24-year-old mother of four, reveals. Irene recently received a letter explaining that she will be losing benefits in twenty-two months. Her former caseworker had "shielded me from the regulations," she says, exempting her time in school from the time clock even though the school she was attending did not qualify as a legitimate training option. Wanda's current caseworker would not exempt the time. "I'm going to try to switch welfare offices by using the address at my mother's other apartment," she says. She is hoping to convince a different caseworker to give her some time to get started again. She is enrolled in a job readiness program but is not currently attending the program, even though it is required to maintain her benefits. "I had to find a babysitter, and the only one I could find charged $100 per day," she claims. "I'm doing OK, I just want twelve months to get myself together without having to attend a number of unhelpful job training programs. If not, I'm not really worried, because my mother covers all of my other expenses. I'm not going to go and get a McDonald's job! Because I know I can't feed my family with that. They're not doing it! That would be stupid of me."

Nurturers are often ineffective at labor market participation and often complain about potential jobs. These complaints justify their low labor force involvement, at least in their own minds. When first interviewed, Latanza, a Nurturer, was trying to get her benefits back. Latanza lost her benefits when her caseworker required her to volunteer and she refused. "They're so screwed up down there. They make you go to school, volunteer, I don't want to volunteer to get aid. I just want to go to school, get a degree or something." Currently she receives only Medicaid. She would like to become a certified nursing assistant and work with the elderly and disabled. "I want to go to school and they won't let me," she says. At the next interview a year later Latanza was still not working or receiving welfare. She was currently waiting to hear about her reapplication. She had also applied for disability because of a health condition that limits her ability to do heavy lifting or any strenuous work. She had received emergency food stamps but was waiting for another round of those. "They are coming way later than the caseworker told me that they should be coming." Without welfare for more than a year now, she agrees it has been hard. "My fiancé brings in the money to buy the groceries and pay the rent. It's hard, but we keep it together."

Nurturers may even refuse welfare benefits if program requirements conflict with child care, as in the case of Mary, a 42-year-old single mother of a 6-year-old son: "I don't go to the job-training programs that welfare offers because they are at the wrong times with my son's school schedule, and I don't trust anyone in the house with my children." Instead, she goes without and patches together a living with food stamps and income from odd jobs.

FIGURE 4.1—Trends in Work among IFS Sample (4th quarter each year except 2003)

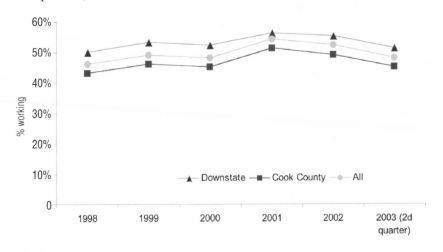

Caseload Trends among the IFS Sample

By June 2003 only 9 percent of the IFS sample was still receiving TANF, according to administrative data on state caseloads. About one-third of IFS respondents in 2003 were still receiving Medicaid and food stamps, which Illinois allowed under its generous work-support philosophy. Nearly one-half (46%) of respondents were receiving no benefits of any kind in 2003, up from 18 percent in 1999. Helping women leave the rolls was a strong economy and a significant expansion of the Earned Income Tax Credit, which can boost certain low-income workers' incomes by $5,000 a year. The EITC has in several studies been shown to encourage work participation (Holt, 2006). The unemployment rate in Illinois declined from 7.6 percent in 1992 to a historic low of 4.3 percent by 1999. Unemployment would begin to rise with the economic slowdown of the early 2000s, however, and was at 6.6 percent in 2003, the last year of the IFS study.

Even with work supports, the large declines in welfare were not matched by comparable increases in work (see figure 4.1). In each of the four study waves, consistently half of the TANF recipients worked for pay at some point. This means that one-half were not working for pay and were no longer receiving TANF. Downstate respondents were more likely than Cook County respondents to be working (63% vs. 46%) and to be no longer receiving TANF (94% vs. 89%). We return to the vulnerable Cook County group at the end of the chapter.

Work and Earnings

Given that half of the IFS sample were not working, and nearly as many were no longer receiving TANF (see below), it is perhaps not too surprising that mean incomes were so low. In 2002 the mean (average) annual income was $14,569. That put 95 percent of respondents in poverty. Granted, income had greatly improved since 1999—roughly doubling, in fact. But the types of jobs the women were finding, and the wages they earned, were often too low to boost them above the poverty line.

The median (typical) wage for employed respondents was $8.58 per hour in 2003, when the minimum wage in the state was $6.50. Not surprising, given their low education (only 59% had completed high school), the majority of employed respondents (84%) worked in services or retail. In 2003 only 30 percent of those employed had employer-sponsored health insurance, up from 16 percent in 1999. Work was also intermittent. Only one-fourth of the women interviewed reported working at the time of each of the four interviews. Almost the same proportion was not working at any of the interviews. Respondents reported holding an average of 1.1 jobs in the previous 12 months, although job retention was rising over the course of the study.

Among women who were working, most were working full-time. The percentage working part-time (24%) held steady between 1999 and 2003, while those working full-time increased slightly from 62 percent in 1999 to 65 percent in 2003. Those working more than full-time (at least 41 hours a week) declined from 14 percent to 10 percent. As time went on, fewer women reported that they would like to work more hours, perhaps reflecting the growing difficulty of juggling parenting responsibilities and the stress of low-wage work. In 1999, 56 percent reported wanting to work more, but that had dropped to 48 percent in 2003. Only about one-fourth were very satisfied with their jobs, a significant decline from 1999.

Geraldine, a Nurturer, captures the sentiment of many with whom we spoke: "I'm getting tired of working in the school cafeteria. . . . I'm still a part-time worker, they don't let me move to a better schedule. The only good thing is that I have a paycheck. But I'm really tired of it. I don't make enough money, I can't even pay my bills with it."

Many studies have found that workers in jobs that pay low wages and offer little flexibility or sense of control face considerably higher stress. Add to that worry about children in care situations, or children left unattended after school, especially in high-crime neighborhoods (see the chapter on child outcomes), and the women in the IFS study were likely under considerable strain. The initial flush of excitement about being in the job force and earning a living may have begun to wear by 2003, as Lillianna, a Striver, reveals: "It's a lot of hours I have to put in for a little part-time job. I get tired, I get stressed out. I don't have any life. I feel like I'm always on the go. I took it because I recently lost my job at [the hotel]. . . . It's hard work. I took it because I needed the income."

It is in attitudes toward and juggling of work that we see distinct differences among our categories of Disaffected, Nurturers, and Strivers. Nurturers often worry that their children would not be cared for properly, or that they will miss out on their children's lives if they worked. Many do not trust caregivers outside of their family. One Nurturer quit her job after coming home to find her child had diaper rash. "My children never had a rash when she was with me."

. Alice is the mother of three children. At the time of the first interview, she was neither working nor receiving welfare. She was trying to obtain benefits again but stated that she did not want to comply with the requirements of going to school or volunteering in a job. One year later, Alice was still not working, nor had she begun receiving benefits again. She had worked at a McDonald's for three days but quit because of the heat and feelings of dizziness.

Tricia, in our Disaffected category, at our interview in 1998 had just been fired from her job in a car wash. "I don't really know what it was about," she says of her firing, "but it was something that was real kind of off the wall. I don't really know. I wasn't going to worry about it." The following year, she remained unemployed, although the car wash had called her back to return to work. But, she says, "I was too proud to return to work for people who had scammed me in the first place." Over the course of the year she applied to various local establishments, to no avail. She currently lives with her mother and does not pay rent. "I help out around the house and do the shopping and cooking. But I'm pissed off because my sisters who live on the first and third floors [of her mother's three-flat] only pay $150 each a month to my mother for rent." In one breath Tricia says, "Once I leave, I'm not coming back, to hell with them all." And in the other she says, "If I weren't living with my mother I don't know what I'd do. I would probably come to a restaurant like this one [where the interview took place] and stand inside until they hired me. I might ask for old food to feed my children. I would make them hire me. I would have to do something."

Charlene, also in the Disaffected category, is doing little to plan for the future, having just quit a job where she was verbally abused "by the president of the company. She degraded me . . . I couldn't take it no more, I think I lost it. Unemployment insurance gives me a little time to pull myself together. They're supposed to find me a job. I can stay on unemployment for six months, if I don't find a job by then they will cut me off. In that case I'll have to go back to public aid."

Others, like Lisa, find the work beneath them, a view opposite from that held by most of the Strivers:

> Finally I humbled myself by taking a job as a packer on a factory line for $6.30 [per hour] when the least I had made before was $10 [per hour]. I really don't want to be in the factory business, I'd rather be in social service work, but this is what I have to do for now. I'm frustrated because I have an education and degrees but still can't get a job in my field. I've worked with the homeless and was homeless myself! People don't want experience these days, they want the paper behind a person [as in their credentials].

Still others lack direction or are unable to form a plan for the future. Ella, for example, reports that she is looking for work but is unable to show how. "I fill out applications, when I hear of job openings," she says. Ella lives with her mother, who owns the house they live in, and pays no rent. Although Ella has a working role model in her mother, she takes little interest in her mother's job—or any job, for that matter. "My mother manages something, I never have known quite what she really does."

Unlike the Disaffected and Nurturers, Strivers less frequently feel the strain of work. Lawanda's job, she says, "is not stressful and brings me a lot of satisfaction. I feel good when my manager tells me that I have done a good job. I'd like to own a barbershop and run my own business. It will probably take me ten years to save the money." Or as Moralisia, another Striver, says, "I'm very happy with my current job and feel for the first time that I've gotten into a professional career track with many possibilities, such as becoming a teacher's assistant or a licensed day care provider or a mentor."

Child Care

Child care was a major concern for many women. In fact, as noted in the prior chapter, the reluctance to leave children with a caregiver often distinguished those who did and did not embrace work. Many women, particularly Nurturers, felt that working while their children were young was harmful, and that they were missing out on important aspects of their children's lives. Grace, a Nurturer, summed it up for many: "I don't mind the working thing, I just don't want to leave my babies. I don't believe in my job taking over my life. I don't need to work. I want to spend quality time with my kids."

Although the state provided child-care subsidies regardless of TANF status for those whose incomes were below 50 percent of the current state median, with a parent copay required, use of these subsidies by respondents declined between 1999 and 2003. By 2003 only one-fourth of respondents with a child under age twelve were using subsidies. Many women spoke of the concern of leaving children in care, as Claribel describes: "The baby is too small, and leaving him with a babysitter would make me worry too much. My sister and mother can take care of the baby if I have a part-time job, but they can't if I work full-time. I won't trust him to someone I don't know."

The data show that women were more likely by far to use extended family members (such as grandparents or aunts) or siblings to care for their children. Nearly six in ten children were cared for by relatives in 2003, a dramatic 17 percentage point increase since 1999. The next most common caregiver was the respondent herself (22%). Fig. 4.2 shows the trends in type of care.

As time went on, child-care arrangements became more stable. Ninety-two percent of children in 2003 had no more than one child-care arrangement in the previous year, up from 89 percent in 1999. Concurrently, the percentage of families with two to three child-care arrangements declined to 8 percent in 2003, from 10 percent in 1999.

Financial Situation

Although earnings were meager, work did indeed pay in Illinois. Those who worked were less likely to experience poverty or material hardship. A key argument among conservative scholars in the lead-up to welfare reform was that women were sometimes better off on welfare than working. Without work requirements and other stipulations, they argued, women—like the infamous Phyllis of Charles Murray's *Losing Ground*—were acting as the rational economic persons they were. To ensure that work paid more than welfare, Illinois built in several work supports that would cushion the transition from welfare to work and make work pay. The federal government did the same; for example, it greatly expanded the Earned Income Tax Credit, which, as already noted, can boost a low-income working family's income by as much as $5,000 annually. The federal EITC is, in fact, the largest antipoverty policy in the country. In 2003 it paid out $34.4 billion to 19.3 million families, up from 15 million families just ten years earlier.[1] Several states, including Illinois, have also created a state EITC, although Illinois's EITC is among the smallest. Initiated nationally in 1975 as a means to reduce the burden of a regressive tax code on the working poor, and greatly expanded in 1990 and again in 1993, the federal program has been credited with lifting millions out of poverty—4.4 million in 2003 alone, more than half of them children. Without the EITC, the poverty rate among children would be 25 percent higher.[2] The EITC supplements low-wage earnings not only by offsetting part or all of income-tax liability but often also by providing a tax refund tied to wages. The amount of credit depends on family size and income.

FIGURE 4.2—Main Type of Child Care Used in Week Preceding Interview (1999–2003)

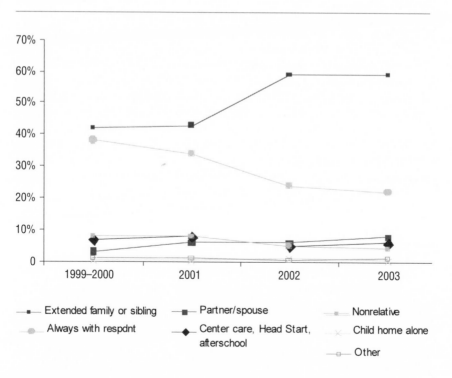

The refund is largest for the lowest earners and phases out with rising income.[3] Among IFS respondents working for pay, 82 percent reported receiving an EITC in 2002.

In addition to the EITC, Illinois extended health care coverage (Medicaid) as low-income women transitioned to the workforce, created child-care subsidies, allowed women to keep more of their welfare checks before benefits were reduced owing to earnings (earnings "disregards"), and stopped the time-limit clock if TANF recipients were working.

These work supports appear to have paid off. Among those working and receiving TANF, mean annual family income (including food stamps, child care, EITC, earnings, and other supports) among IFS respondents was $14,742 in 2003. Among those relying solely on work, earnings were even higher, at $17,941. In comparison, in 2003 the annual average income of those not working but still receiving TANF was $12,518 and of those neither working nor receiving TANF was $12,730.

The difference of several thousand dollars a year in wages mattered significantly to the women. Earnings among all the women, even those relying solely on work, were low. Every penny mattered, as Maria, a Striver, suggests:

> It's very difficult. . . . I'm usually left with $50 that has to stretch. The rent here is $500, and this is not a nice neighborhood! . . . What am I going to do? I stretch my money. My kids want stuff, they want to go somewhere, but I can't go. My $50 is for gas. And now I've got a new car, my mother doesn't work anymore. I wish at least they would give me food stamps. I spend $200 in food for the five people living in the house.

Although many are struggling, the added income can mean the difference between having something left over and seeking out a food pantry. "I feel really good about my work," says Sabrina, a Striver. "I do more and accomplish more. The way [my children] look at me makes a difference. If they ask for a dollar, I can give it to them."

Others have seen more considerable increases and are reaping the benefits. Yvondelyne, a Striver, earns about $1,600 a month, which allows her to save for the future for the first time:

> Before taxes I make about $400 a week. I have $18 a week taken out for medical, and I also pay union dues. I get $42 a month in food stamps. I get $14 every two weeks in child support, and my caseworker called me to see if I had left out a zero. I think it's funny how little I get, but I don't complain. I've been putting money into a 401(k) plan; every week they take $15 out of my paycheck, and then the company doubles it.

Melody is a 29-year-old Striver and mother of two. She is working full-time and will soon be eligible for company benefits. On welfare she received approximately $300 per month, or $3,600 a year, plus food stamps and Medicaid. Today she earns about $13,000 a year. Her earnings increase of about $10,000 pre- and post-welfare—double the $5,000 gap between the highest and lowest earners above—shows what a cushion allows. Melody has a savings account and feels secure for the first time. "You do the math," she says.

Shannon, another Striver, also has a savings account for the first time. "My pay will increase by $7,000 more a year. My brother told me to pay myself like I pay my bills every month so that I can save money. I've paid myself $30 every month before paying any bills since then."

Despite increases in work, earnings, and (in some cases like those above) savings, most respondents perceived their financial situation to be about the same over the four-year period. And that situation was precarious for many. About 85 percent said they worry a lot about having enough money in the future. About one-half reported material hardship, although that number had dropped considerably since the beginning of reform. Homelessness and food insecurity saw modest declines, yet 7 percent worried that their children were not eating enough because they did not have enough money for food.

Here again, though, work seems to pay. The TANF-only group reported the highest levels of material hardship, with those working and receiving TANF close behind (see table 4.1 and figure 4.3).

Health and Well-Being

Mental and physical health had improved over the course of the study. By 2003 the proportion of respondents reporting depressive symptoms had declined to 18 percent, down from 24 percent in 1999. The increased self-esteem from work, coupled with a steady routine, may have helped improve depressive symptoms among some. The added stresses of balancing work and family on meager wages, however, might have prevented even greater improvement in mental health. In addition, continued insurance coverage likely helped maintain health among the women and their children. Health insurance, thanks to the state's allowing former TANF recipients to keep Medicaid while they transitioned into the workforce, was seldom an issue for the respondents. Medicaid remained the most common form of health insurance, with 65 percent of the sample covered by the public program in 2003. This had declined from 73 percent in 1999, reflecting the growing participation in the workforce. Employer-sponsored health coverage, while still low, doubled, from 8 percent in 1999 to 16 percent in 2003. Roughly the same percentage had no coverage in 1999 as in 2003 (18%). This compares with the national statistic of 16.6 percent of Americans lacking health insurance in 2005.

TABLE 4.1—Material Hardship in 2003 by Work and TANF Status

	No Work/ No TANF	*Work Only*	*Combining Work and TANF*	*TANF Only*
Phone service turned off	32%	20%	24%	39%
Gas/electricity turned off	5	8	19	11
Could not pay full rent/ mortgage	10	8	14	9
Evicted	3	2	5	6
Respondent or child needed to see doctor but couldn't afford to go	14	12	0	4
Moved in with others to reduce expenses	8	3	5	11
One or more of the above hardships	49	40	43	53
Three or more of the above hardships	15	13	10	9
Went to church or charity for clothes/financial help	8	5	14	13
Worried that children were not eating enough because not enough money for food	8	5	0	10
Homeless	2	3	5	4

*** $p < 0.001$; ** $p < 0.01$; * $p < 0.05$, chi-square tests

Sanctions

Sanctions were an important policy tool in welfare reform, putting some teeth into the rules. In many states, including Illinois, sanctions were graduated, with the recipient having an opportunity to return to the rolls if she complied with rules and requirements. Illinois has a moderate, three-step sanction process that becomes more severe as noncompliance persists. At the first instance of noncompliance, the state cuts cash

FIGURE 4.3—Material Hardship by Work Status

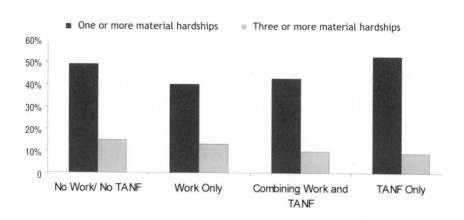

benefits in half until the recipient complies with the rules or shows good cause for failing to do so. A second infraction reduces the welfare check in half again for three months or until the recipient complies. These two sanctions are "partial grant" sanctions. A third offense results in a full sanction—that is, the family loses the entire welfare check. Although Illinois's sanction policy was more generous than that of some states, the message was clear: We mean business, and welfare is no longer a free ride. (For more on sanctions, see Chapter 8.)

In Illinois, more than one-third of the IFS sample (36%) were sanctioned at some point between 1999 and 2003. Most of the sanctions were partial. Full cutoffs were extremely rare. After increasing initially, the use of sanctions has leveled off. In 1999, 13 percent of respondents experienced a sanction, compared with 23 percent of respondents in 2000, 2001, or 2002 (2003 data were not available at the time of the final IFS report). Sanctioned respondents, on average, had more children, had more children with health issues, and were more likely to have participated in a job-search program. Those who had received sanctions also reported more material hardship than those who avoided sanctions. Sanctioned families more often moved in with others, doubling up to save money.

How Are the Most Vulnerable Families Faring?

In 2003, 43 percent of respondents were neither working nor receiving TANF. The size of this group had risen dramatically from 1999, when it was 17 percent (see figure 4.4). This steady increase in a group that is vulnerable to poverty and hardship requires further attention from researchers and policy makers. Many of these women were relying on informal sources of support or government benefits other than TANF. This group also reported high rates of material hardship and health problems.

The majority of this group fell into the Nurturer and Disaffected categories. Of the sixty women interviewed in depth in 1999, twelve were not working, and twenty-three reported no income from work in the previous year. Of those not working, 58 percent were Nurturers, 15 percent were Strivers, and 14 percent were Disaffected. Joan, in our Disaffected category, was neither receiving welfare nor working. Nor was she looking for work. She manages, she reports, "with the grace of God, his blessing." Her source of support is "Father God and my fiancé. He's my soul mate." Her fiancé repairs cars for friends and others. Joan ultimately wants to run a shelter for neglected children and a kitchen for "hungry battered women."

Another vulnerable group is those relying only on TANF, who were 9 percent of the sample in 2003. This group has not yet made the jump to the workforce for a variety of reasons, including mental illness and severe educational shortfalls. Many are likely approaching time limits on TANF, although our data do not reveal the exact number. Among all IFS respondents, however, 36 percent had used more than half of their possible time. Those who already had used half their time were more likely to be unemployed, to be receiving a subsidy for housing, to have health problems, and to have been on welfare for a longer period. Although the first five-year time limit occurred in 2001 (five years after 1996), nearly all the families in

FIGURE 4.4—Change Over Time in Percentage of Those Neither Working Nor Receiving Welfare and Those Receiving Tanf

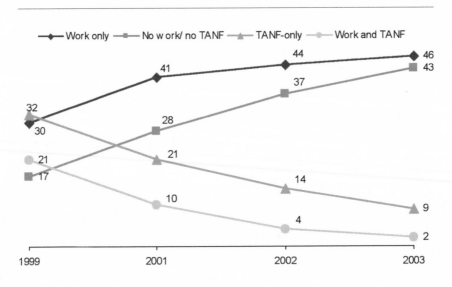

our sample had managed to "save" some of their TANF eligibility by leaving welfare temporarily or permanently (or by entering the workforce, which stops the clock in Illinois). However, these families eventually will reach their limit, and those with health or mental health impairments, or other serious barriers to work, will likely meet them first.

table 4.2 shows the demographic characteristics of respondents based on their work and welfare status as of 2003. Those who had left welfare without a job were more likely to be older, have less education, and be from Cook County.

As noted, those neither working nor receiving TANF, and those relying solely on TANF, are more vulnerable. Forty-six percent of the former reported material hardship in the past year, and 54 percent of the TANF-only group reported hardship, including being evicted, having utilities shut off, being unable to afford a doctor, or related problems. Nine percent of the no work/no TANF group and 12 percent of the TANF-only group reported worrying that their children were not eating because of lack of money. Twelve percent of those neither working nor receiving TANF reported that their children needed to see a doctor, but they couldn't afford to take them. This was the case for less than 1 percent of the TANF-only group, reflecting the higher Medicaid coverage among this group.

The two groups also had more health problems, which boded ill for their future employability and financial security. Nonemployed women who'd left the welfare rolls were significantly more likely, at 27 percent, than employed leavers (11%) to rate their health as fair or poor. The TANF-only group reported similar rates of poor health.

How do these women survive? We asked several questions about alternative sources of support, such as spouses or boyfriends, informal work, charity, and other government programs. We find that marriage and cohabitation were fairly common among nonemployed women no longer receiving TANF. Ten percent were currently married, and 12 percent were cohabiting. These rates are only slightly lower than those in the group that was working and combining TANF (17%), and nearly identical to the TANF-only and work-only groups. None of these differences are statistically significant, however. Many others relied on boyfriends to cover living expenses; about one-third of the group neither working nor receiving TANF, and one-fifth of the TANF-only group, relied on a boyfriend.

Several of the women (about 30%) relied on informal work, while similar proportions borrowed money from family and friends. About one-fifth of the TANF-only group relied on charity, and nearly half used a food pantry or soup kitchen. Of those neither working nor receiving welfare, 11 percent relied on charity and 17 percent had been to a food pantry. These two groups were significantly more likely to use these resources than were those working or combining work with TANF. Food stamps and Medicaid were also vital to these women, as were other programs, such as Supplemental

TABLE 4.2—Demographic Characteristics of IFS Sample in 2003
by Welfare and Work Status

	No Work/ No TANF	Work Only	Combining Work and TANF	TANF Only
High school diploma or GED (%)*** [1, 3]	51	68	47	52
Mean age**[1]	32.5	30.8	35.3	31
Race-ethnicity (%)				
African American	84	87	87	83
White	13	13	13	13
Other	3	0	0	5
Hispanic	13	13	13	10
Number of children	2.6	2.4	3.1	2.6
Has child under age 5 (%)	52	56	43	54
Married (%)**[2,4]	7	9	27	2
Cook County (%)*[1]	93	87	87	96
Downstate (%)	7	13	13	4

[1] = No work/no TANF significantly different from work-only
[2] = No work/ no TANF significantly different from work/TANF
[3] = Work-only significantly different from TANF-only
[4] = Work/TANF significantly different from TANF-only
* $p < 0.05$; ** $p < 0.01$; *** $p < 0.001$

Security Insurance (disability insurance). Participation in these ancillary programs has risen over time among these two groups.

The Two Worlds of Welfare

More than six years after welfare reform, Illinois has witnessed a significant decline in its welfare caseload, but with no accompanying rise in labor force participation. Employment rates of our sample remained at approximately 50 percent throughout the four years of the IFS study.

Increasing numbers of respondents were surviving (often barely) without either welfare or a job. The result is a distinct divide into two worlds: those working and those not.

Those who do work appear to be faring as well as or better than they did prior to reform, thanks to strong work supports in the state, as well as a higher minimum wage than in many states. Those unable to work are often struggling. Some are still receiving TANF, with a clock ticking. A much larger group is on their own without a net or a job. This group is relying on informal work and community and family charity to get by. Hardship is high, and health and well-being are at risk. They view the welfare system not as reformers intended but as either a new hassle in their lives to circumvent, as many of the Nurturers do, or as a sometimes confusing set of new, difficult requirements, as the Disaffected do.

Even among those working, poverty is high and finances are precarious. Many women do enjoy their jobs, however, and find a reward in earning a paycheck. These women, largely Strivers, have used the welfare system as it was intended—as a tool to propel them toward self-sufficiency.

These profiles of welfare and the women bound to the program are instructive not just as added flavor to the statistics but as an important tool in discerning the effects of policy changes and ultimately designing better policy. Person-based policy underscores the individuality of people and their approaches to life. Policies that overlook these individual nuances will undoubtedly miss the mark and leave a large segment of low-income women behind in a post-welfare world. The following chapters will look more in depth at what distinguishes these two worlds of welfare, identifying predictors of success and struggle.

CHAPTER 5

Working and Earning After Welfare Reform

AS NOTED IN THE PREVIOUS CHAPTER, a significant portion of IFS participants was not working several years after welfare reform. This chapter moves beyond overview trends and examines which personal and other factors predict work and earnings among our sample. If past research is any indication, those with more "human capital" (education, work skills, lack of barriers) should do better in the labor force. The conservative argument prior to welfare reform would have predicted that those who had been on welfare for longer periods would likely fare more poorly in the labor market, given the supposed disincentive that welfare created. Ideology aside, the research on this is more mixed, however.

Study Design

To measure labor force participation, we examined administrative data from the Unemployment Insurance system (UI data) at each interview wave (annually from 1999 to 2003) and also surveyed the women themselves, asking them to estimate in how many months they had worked at least ten hours per week during the previous year or since their last interview.[1] Employers are required to report all earnings quarterly to the UI. By matching Social Security numbers to the earnings reports, we were able to gauge earnings in our sample. We summed pretax earnings in the four quarters before each survey to yield a measure of annual income from work.

To predict the factors that are likely to affect work and earnings, we conducted two analyses: a cross-sectional analysis using a Tobit model[2] to adjust for potential oversight of earnings of individuals not in the workforce ("left-censored" data) and a longitudinal analysis that gauges whether earnings and employment are changing over time, while simultaneously accounting for random effects of change over time.[3] The variables that are likely to affect employment and earnings are grouped into five major categories.

The first category includes human capital variables: educational attainment, job-related skills, and health status. The second category is nonwage income: formal and informal child support, and financial support for living expenses from a spouse or partner, or a government rent subsidy. On the one hand, high levels of support may lower the likelihood of working. On the other hand, such support may relieve the stress of making ends meet and function as an incentive to continue working. As the third category we include a set of neighborhood characteristics (measured using census tract data) that can influence work, including average income in the neighborhood and the unemployment rate. According to some theories, both higher neighborhood income and lower unemployment should encourage our sample members to work and earn more. As William Julius Wilson argued in the *Truly Disadvantaged*, and scores of other social scientists investigated in urban ethnographies, neighborhood conditions can keep people from overcoming poverty. High rates of joblessness and poverty in a neighborhood, Wilson argued, cut people off from the networks and social connections that lead to jobs. Working role models dry up as well. As Mickey Kaus, a thoughtful early proponent of welfare reform, put it, when a mom sets her alarm clock, the children will set theirs (DeParle, 2006).

The fourth group of explanatory variables includes demographic characteristics such as race-ethnicity, age, marital status, and having at least one child under the age of three. Race differences in labor market participation and performance between minority and majority groups are well documented (Smith & Welch, 1989; O'Neill, 1990). We expect that African Americans will have lower labor force participation and earnings on average than whites or Hispanics. We expect married individuals to be more likely to work and earn potentially higher incomes (Korenman & Neumark, 1991). We expect that caregivers with young children will be less likely to work and will earn less than those with older children.

The fifth group of explanatory variables includes factors such as time on welfare, family hardship, housing expenses, informal work status, and region of residence. Time on welfare is measured using administration data and includes the total months the respondent received welfare between February 1980 and the sampling period in fall 1998. We expect longer-term welfare receipt to limit labor force participation and earnings. This latter relationship has been the subject of debate for many years, and the evidence is coming down on the disincentive side. In very rigorous studies, Moffitt (1992) and Danziger and colleagues (1981) both found that public welfare reduces work effort. As for the other variables, we expect high housing costs to be associated with increased work and earnings. In contrast, we expect that those who work informally and those who reside in Cook County (which includes Chicago) will be less likely to work in the official labor market and will have lower earnings. Note that higher earnings do not necessarily indicate higher hourly wages. They may simply result from working more hours per week for longer periods of time.

Descriptive Statistics

On average, the individuals in our sample participated in the labor force approximately half a year (see table 5.1), with little variation over time. Somewhat more than 30 percent of our sample was not working. The average earnings across the four interviews ranged from approximately $5,000 to $7,000. Both earnings and time in the workforce align with past research on reform. Most recently, Jeffrey Grogger and Lynn Karoly, in an overview of several post-welfare studies, find that welfare reform raised earnings only minimally. The most successful program, they report, raised annual earnings by less than $2,200. The next most successful program raised earnings by about $1,000 (Grogger & Karoly, 2005). However, as we noted, even modest amounts can make a sizable difference in small household budgets. The impact, in other words, is relative. That said, the incomes of many former welfare recipients remain stubbornly close to poverty thresholds.

The majority had a high school degree (table 5.1) and job skills. The percentage with a high school degree and job skills increased over time. Nearly one in four was in poor health or had a chronic health problem. Approximately one-half of respondents received formal or informal child support, and approximately one in five across all four sampling waves received financial support from a spouse or partner for living expenses. Overall, most respondents lived in low-income, high-unemployment neighborhoods. On average, our sample was in their early thirties with two to three children. The majority of individuals were not married or cohabitating and, on average, had spent approximately 6.5 years on welfare.

table 5.2 summarizes work status and welfare use for all four waves. The proportion of people who were relying only on welfare (and not working) at the time of the survey decreased dramatically over time. It is equally noteworthy, however, that the proportion of those who left welfare without a job more than doubled during the study time span. Clearly those who leave welfare do not always leave for jobs. Also worth noting is

TABLE 5.1—Profiles of Sample

Variables of Interest	Interview 1, 1999–2000	Interview 2, 2001	Interview 3, 2002	Interview 4, 2003
Number of participants	1363	1183	1072	967
Number of months in the labor force	5.9	6.0	6.1	5.5
Number of months could have worked	12.0	14.2	12.1	12.0
Earnings	$4,867	5,751	6,462	6,748
Human capital				
High school degree	58.9%	71.0%	71.5%	72.6%
Job skills	70.7%	71.6%	72.6%	72.9%
Poor health	31.9%	25.3%	22.4%	24.1%
Nonwage income				
Child support	48.9%	55.0%	57.0%	58.5%
Financial support	19.9%	26.8%	27.9%	30.5%
Housing subsidy	25.5%	22.0%	25.0%	30.3%
Neighborhood characteristics				
Average annual income	$29,593	$30,980	$30,590	$30,650
Percent unemployment	18.0%	16.9%	16.9%	16.7%
Demographic characteristics				
Black	78.0%	78.2%	79.1%	78.2%
Hispanic	11.8%	12.7%	12.2%	12.5%
White	8.2%	7.4%	7.1%	7.4%
Age	31.7	32.6	33.7	34.6
Married or living together	16.0%	18.7%	18.8%	20.8%
Number of children	2.5	2.6	2.6	2.7
Controls				
Time on welfare (months)	77.1	78.0	79.0	78.1
Informal work	29.2%	26.3%	21.0%	21.6%

Note: Data are weighted in all analyses to adjust for nonproportional sampling between Cook County and the rest of the state and differences in nonresponse rates across various groups.

the decreasing proportion of the sample who combine work and welfare, from 21 percent in 1998 to 2 percent in 2003. As noted in Chapter 2, Illinois stops the clock for those welfare recipients who are working thirty hours a week. It is therefore surprising that almost none of the IFS sample were combining work and welfare by 2003 and thereby taking advantage of having their clock stopped in terms of preserving their eligibility for TANF benefits.

Influences on Work and Earnings

As expected, individuals with a high school degree are more likely to be in the labor force for longer periods of time than individuals with lower levels of education, even after holding all other likely impacts on employment constant (such as time on welfare, race, etc.). The same effect is apparent for job skills. In other words, among otherwise identical persons, those with more education and job skills are more likely to be working. Again, this is not surprising, given the importance of both in the job market. In fact, few of the measures bucked conventional expectations: poor health, race-ethnicity, family hardship, residence in urban Cook County, and having at least one child under the age of three were all associated with less work, holding all else constant (see table 5.3).

Interestingly, receiving a housing subsidy increased the likelihood of working.[4] Recipients in 1999–2000 who received a subsidy were 10 percent more likely to be working than those who were paying full price for rent. The effect of housing subsidies became more important over time. By 2003 those with a subsidy were 17 percent more likely to be working. Housing

Table 5.2—Work Status and Welfare Use

	Interview 1, 1999–2000	Interview 2, 2001	Interview 3, 2002	Interview 4, 2003
Number of participants	1363	1183	1072	967
Work only	29.8%	42.5%	44.7%	46.2%
Work and welfare	20.6%	10.4%	4.2%	1.5%
Welfare only	31.5%	20.4%	14.3%	9.1%
No work/no welfare	18.1%	26.6%	36.8%	43.0%

Note: Percentages do not always sum to 100% because of rounding.

TABLE 5.3— Human Capital, Neighborhood, and Demographic Characteristics That Predict Labor Force Participation (Tobit, cross-sectional analysis)

	PROPORTION OF MONTHS IN THE LABOR FORCE							
	Wave 1		Wave 2		Wave 3		Wave 4	
Independent Variables	*Estimate*	*SE*	*Estimate*	*SE*	*Estimate*	*SE*	*Estimate*	*SE*
Human capital								
High school degree	0.082	0.032	0.117	0.039	0.227	0.041	0.194	0.049
Job skills	0.089	0.034	-0.030	0.039	0.038	0.041	0.085	0.049
Poor health	-0.112	0.033	-0.159	0.042	-0.012	0.045	-0.312	0.054
Nonwage income								
Child support	0.016	0.031	-0.070	0.035	-0.002	0.037	0.017	0.044
Financial support	0.040	0.041	-0.030	0.044	0.116	0.047	-0.047	0.053
Housing subsidy	0.105	0.037	0.154	0.043	0.110	0.045	0.172	0.054
Neighborhood characteristics								
Average income >$40,000	0.033	0.040	0.015	0.047	0.027	0.050	0.038	0.060
Percent unemployment	-0.385	0.173	-0.438	0.224	0.155	0.229	0.516	0.281
Demographic characteristics								
White	-0.036	0.048	-0.007	0.071	-0.009	0.074	0.042	0.086
Hispanic	0.152	0.060	-0.029	0.054	0.100	0.058	0.026	0.069
Other race/ethnicity	-0.131	0.154	-0.573	0.167	-0.386	0.160	-0.986	0.230
Age: linear term	0.050	0.014	0.028	0.016	0.034	0.018	0.046	0.023
Age: quadratic term	-0.0007	0.0002	-0.0005	0.0002	-0.0006	0.0002	-0.0007	0.0003
Married or living together	-0.079	0.046	0.113	0.050	-0.171	0.056	0.045	0.023
One child <3 years old	-0.024	0.041	-0.182	0.039	-0.181	0.043	-0.126	0.049
Controls								
Nine or more years on welfare	0.007	0.035	-0.037	0.041	-0.037	0.041	-0.042	0.051
Family hardship	-0.051	0.030	-0.118	0.034	-0.118	0.035	-0.004	0.043
Housing expenses	0.0005	0.0001	0.0006	0.0001	0.0005	0.0001	0.0007	0.0001
Region: Cook County vs. downstate	-0.245	0.052	-0.107	0.061	-0.258	0.063	-0.348	0.074

TABLE 5.4—Human Capital, Neighborhood, and Demographic Characteristics That Predict Earnings (Tobit, cross-sectional analysis)

LOG EARNINGS

Independent Variables	Wave 1 Estimate	SE	Wave 2 Estimate	SE	Wave 3 Estimate	SE	Wave 4 Estimate	SE
Human capital								
High school degree	1.375	0.369	0.316	0.398	1.360	0.487	1.888	0.566
Job skills	0.255	0.396	0.899	0.401	0.125	0.488	1.218	0.564
Poor health	-1.230	0.390	-2.040	0.441	-1.179	0.542	-1.499	0.621
Neighborhood characteristics								
Average income > $40,000	1.677	0.474	1.477	0.487	0.462	0.589	0.111	0.688
Percent unemployment	0.377	1.984	-2.125	2.290	-3.759	2.741	0.423	3.252
Demographic characteristics								
White	0.285	0.685	-0.990	0.741	-1.547	0.862	-0.205	0.957
Hispanic	0.946	0.567	-0.035	0.554	-0.030	0.681	0.711	0.784
Other race/ethnicity	-13.445	2.613	-9.817	2.093	-5.069	2.008	-10.527	2.629
Age: linear term	0.447	0.167	0.321	0.166	0.352	0.208	0.120	0.264
Age: quadratic term	-0.007	0.002	-0.005	0.002	-0.006	0.003	-0.003	0.004
Married or living together	-0.039	0.485	-0.616	0.455	-0.216	0.544	-0.672	0.627
One child <3 years old	-0.928	0.472	-1.962	0.391	-1.169	0.505	-0.753	0.557
Controls								
Nine or more years on welfare	-0.778	0.406	-0.554	0.419	-0.574	0.490	0.936	0.581
Family hardship	-0.455	0.358	-1.043	0.353	-0.884	0.422	-0.636	0.497
Housing expenses	0.002	0.001	0.002	0.001	0.004	0.001	0.004	0.001
Informal work	-1.130	0.391	-1.217	0.410	-2.662	0.544	-3.014	0.637
Region: Cook County vs. downstate	-0.604	0.613	-0.910	0.633	-1.030	0.759	-1.506	0.863

support, along with health, living outside of Chicago, and family hardship, had in fact the largest effect on work among the many factors examined.

One finding that parted from expectations was time on welfare. We found that being on welfare for nine years or more did not affect labor force participation. This is a very important finding given the emphasis that Murray and other conservatives placed on the disastrous effect of long-term welfare receipt, especially on working.

It should be noted that none of these associations imply that the characteristic caused the effect. For example, having a high school degree is only correlated with labor force participation. We are not claiming a cause-and-effect relationship.

Earnings followed similar patterns: Education, job skills, good health, living in higher-income neighborhoods, age, and having fewer young children are all associated with higher earnings (see table 5.4). The strongest predictors of higher earnings were being Asian or some race other than black or Hispanic, having older children, being in good health, and not doing informal work. Time on welfare did not affect earnings. Unlike with labor market participation, we found few notable regional differences in earnings.

Changes in Earnings and Work over Time

The above results are reported at particular points in time—at the time of the annual interview. We also looked at the findings across time (longitudinally) to detect any changing trends in the patterns. The results suggest that the individuals in our sample worked longer periods as time went by. This may be because more individuals were employed over time. Educational attainment at the outset of the study in 1999 is positively associated with longer employment and greater earnings over time, indicating that high school graduates are more likely to participate in the labor force for longer periods of time than others with less education, and to earn more over the course of four years. Health was also a significant predictor of work over time: healthy individuals worked longer periods over time than less healthy individuals. It had no effect on earnings, however. Receiving a housing subsidy also increased the duration of employment over time. Interestingly, higher housing expenses were associated both with longer periods of employment and higher earnings over time. Being on welfare nine or more years had no effect on duration of employment or on earnings over time—just as we found in looking at labor force participation. None of the other variables had statistically significant effects.

In a separate analysis we found that, on average, IFS sample members experienced a mean growth in income between 2000 and 2002 of $3,364 per year, leading to an average income of $14,343. Here, respondents' background characteristics explain very little of the growth (less than 5%). What mattered more was initial income at the first interview (see table 5.5). The higher the income at the first interview, the less income growth over the study period. Controlling for background and neighborhood characteristics, the average individual with $7,798 in income at the first interview earned an additional $3,364 per year. (The background characteristics included race, respondent's age at the birth of her first child, number of children and whether the children were younger or older, and respondent's work, education, and years on welfare.) In contrast, the average individual with initial household income of $15,275 saw no income growth. This $15,000 is very close to the annual income from a full-time job that paid $8 per hour. Those with initial incomes of greater than $15,275 saw income decline over the study period. Thus, our analyses suggest a ceiling effect on income growth in the IFS sample.[5] Those with the lowest incomes experienced the most growth, while those with higher incomes topped out and began to see income loss at some point.

Although the dramatic gain in sample members' incomes is impressive, the low-income ceiling is troubling and should prompt serious concerns about the long-term welfare of these families. The apparent $16,000 ceiling was below the federally established poverty threshold for a family of four (the average respondent has three children) at the time of the study. Moreover, it was less than half of the $38,625 median household income in Chicago in 2000.

The Survival of the Fittest in a TANF World?

Perhaps the most surprising finding was that, controlling for other human capital factors, time on welfare is not associated with labor force participation or earnings. This important finding indicates that, among our sample in Illinois, long-term welfare use has little, if any, significant effect on the likelihood of participating or doing well in the labor market. Although this finding is contrary to the expectations of conservative analysts, it is consistent with more recent research on former welfare participants (Cancian et al., 2002). This finding is also consistent with Blank's (1997) argument that long-term AFDC receipt did not destroy all motivation to work. We return to this topic in the next chapter.

The findings that human capital (education, job skills, health, and other factors) increases work and earnings, although not surprising, have important policy implications, suggesting that investments in education and health can have long-term payoffs in employment and earnings. The same is true for housing subsidies. The results suggest that government housing subsidies can enhance labor force participation and earnings. Policy

TABLE 5.5—Relationship of Wave 1 Income-to-Income Growth

	Sample Mean *(standard deviation)*
Third interview income	$14,343 (459) ***
Annual income growth (slope, at mean wave 1 level)	$3,364 (269) ***
Effect of wave 1 income on growth	-.45 (.02)***
Wave 1 mean income	
Point at which wave 1 household income would	$7,798
experience no income growth (zero slope point)	$15,275

⁺*p* <= 0.10, **p* <= 0.05, ***p* <= 0.01, ****p* <= 0.001

makers should therefore be aware that the current efforts to reduce federal housing assistance may have the unintended consequence of reducing work effort. Our finding that mothers who have young children are less likely to participate and perform well in the labor market than mothers with older children may also point to the need for better child-care options. If our interviews are any indication, women are more comfortable leaving their children in the care of relatives or others whom they know. Support for these caregivers might extend working mothers' care options, and in turn encourage work.

We also detected potentially important regional differences; those residing in more urban Cook County are typically less likely to participate in the labor force than individuals who live in more rural or less urban counties in downstate Illinois. This suggests that regional differences go beyond the economic climate (we control for the unemployment rate), major living expenses (we control for the cost of housing), and race. The Chicago-downstate comparison may very well capture the convergence of the city's heavy reliance on public housing that isolates many welfare recipients in highly stigmatized communities and the extremely segregated nature of its neighborhoods. It may also indirectly measure the spatial mismatch between job requirements and welfare recipients' skills, as more jobs locate in the suburbs, far from transportation lines (Allard & Danziger, 2003).

An important finding is that there is an increase in labor-force participation but not in earnings over time. A primary goal of welfare reform is to increase self-sufficiency through work; however, it is unlikely that working half the year earning approximately $6,000 on average is enough to meet that goal. In fact, 95 percent of the IFS sample was living in poverty in 2003. Other studies have found similar results. Acs & Loprest (2001), for example, found sporadic work in the year after leaving welfare (with only about one-third working in all four quarters) and mean earnings among those employed of about $2,600 per quarter.

Within the intellectual framework created by AFDC, it may have appeared that welfare receipt was causing individuals to stay out of the labor market. Now that we don't have AFDC on which to pin responsibility, it becomes clearer that perhaps the program itself was not completely to blame. When cash assistance disappears, person-centered factors (human capital) become increasingly important in explaining work and earnings. The challenge of attaining self-sufficiency remains when cash assistance disappears. The supposed disincentive has been removed, yet many people still are not working. In our sample, almost one-half (43%) are neither working nor receiving welfare. In this TANF world, personal resources become more visible and identifiable as factors in explaining who works and how much they make. We can identify the role of personal resources in explaining economic effort and outcomes. In other words, when barriers to equality such as the old welfare system are removed, individual differences become more visible and important.

Welfare reform removed AFDC, which was thought to create dependency and a disincentive to work. Nearly a decade later, those poor who have moved into the labor force have improved their economic situations only minimally. Many remain poor. For those not working, the safety net is gone, leaving them and their children in precarious positions. Those starting out with more capital end up with literally more capital. Those least equipped, in contrast, are at risk of being left behind.

These results fill out the portrait presented in the last chapter. There we saw two worlds of welfare emerging, one in which women were leaving welfare for work, using the work supports effectively during their transition into the workforce and making small strides on the road to self-sufficiency. This was countered, however, by a sizable group that was neither working nor receiving welfare, one growing increasingly vulnerable and facing mounting hardship. The findings presented here add some details about their lives, showing that those who are leaving welfare for work are more likely to be those most able to do so: they have the education, job skills, better health, older children, and generally more economic and social cushions. Those who are still on welfare or who have left it without finding a job, or whose job is low-paying and sporadic, are more likely to have severe health problems, live in poorer neighborhoods (more likely in Chicago), and have young children and greater family hardship. What matters little, in the end, is their welfare history. Welfare for these least-prepared women may indeed have been a necessary safety net. Without further job training, education, flexible child care, or mental health and other health services, their prospects are dim in this TANF world.

CHAPTER 6

Depression and Welfare

AS THE PREVIOUS CHAPTER SHOWED, human capital matters in a post-AFDC world. One critical aspect of human capital is health, including mental health. Research has consistently found depression to be prevalent among welfare recipients and other low-income populations (Olson & Pavetti, 1996; Quint, Bos, & Polit, 1997; Zedlewski, 1999). Estimates of the incidence of depression vary widely depending on how depression is measured and the sample used, but it is generally thought that between one-fourth and one-third of welfare recipients suffer from symptoms of depression, compared with about one-fifth of the general population (Derr, Hill, & Pavetti, 2000). In a recent study of poor women in urban areas, Polit, London, & Martinez (2001) reported that almost one-half of welfare recipients suffered depressive symptoms. In a study of current and recent welfare recipients in Michigan, Danziger and colleagues (2000) found that one-fourth of their sample suffered from a major depressive disorder, which is nearly twice as high as among women of comparable ages in national studies (13% reported depressive symptoms). They also found that those who reported symptoms of depression were significantly less likely to be working than other former welfare recipients (38% vs. 55%).

Stress, particularly chronic or enduring stress, is an important factor in the higher rates of depression among low-income individuals (Kessler, 1997; Stueve, Dohrenwend, & Skodol, 1998; Tennant, 2002). Chronic stressors such as poverty, hardship, and a general lack of resources weigh heavily on people's lives. Work-related stresses also play a role in depression. Working in an occupation with little control or autonomy, such as on factory lines or in much of the service sector, has been shown to contribute to depression (Griffin et al., 2002). Lack of work can also contribute to depression (Kessler et al., 2003; Tausig, 1999). In the welfare debate, liberals and conservatives view depression differently. For instance, let's take the two representatives of those positions whom we discussed at length in Chapter 2. In the liberal lexicon, depression and other mental health problems are disabilities that "cause" poverty. Ellwood sees them as barriers that must be overcome before the person can compete in the labor market. For Murray, depression is subsumed under the panoply of problems that are produced by the culture that grows around AFDC and related policies. While Murray does not discuss clinical depression per se, he does suggest that withdrawn and negative points of view are part of blame-the-system thinking and dependency that AFDC stimulates. In this view a life of work and inclusion will improve the mental health of the person who has left welfare behind. For the liberal, depression must be combated before the person can go to work. For the conservative, work will help lift the veil of depression and should be supported as a healing activity. Against this background, we turn to an analysis of depression among our longitudinal sample of welfare recipients.

Although the prevalence of mental health issues is quite high among the poor and welfare populations, few seek mental health services. Jayakody & Stauffer (2000), using data from a survey of individuals with substance abuse issues (which fall under the mental-health umbrella), found that in the previous year only 6 percent of single mothers in their sample had received mental health treatment even though 17 percent had experienced a problem. Research finds little systematic effort among welfare agencies to identify the mental health problems of their clients or to refer recipients for treatment (Derr et al., 2000; Jayakody & Stauffer, 2000).[1]

With the advent of TANF and its work mandates, a growing body of research has examined the relation between work and depression among current and former welfare recipients (Danziger, Kalil, & Anderson, 2000; Jayakody & Stauffer, 2000; Michalopoulos, Schwartz, & Adams-Ciardullo, 2000). Although these studies suggest that depression often leads to less work, the direction of causation is unknown. On the one hand, work may help alleviate mental illness and its symptoms; several studies have shown that work can provide psychological, economic, and attitudinal benefits (Cunningham, Wolbert, & Brockmeier, 2000). As Van Dongen (1996) notes, mentally ill individuals can benefit from work because it provides a distraction from their symptoms, needed structure, an opportunity for socialization, and meaningful activity. On the other hand, the stress of work may contribute to mental illness. Obviously, the degree of impairment is central. The severity of depression falls along a continuum, and those with more serious depression will likely be affected more profoundly in their ability to work.

Below we examine how depression affects work effort by the women in the IFS study. Specifically, we ask which factors distinguish women with depressive symptoms who work from those who do not. We use a regression analysis that allows us to hold constant personal and other factors, such as education levels, that might influence work effort. Between two identical women, both suffering from depression, we identify which factors in their lives promote work and which impede it. We interlace this analysis with quotes from our qualitative interviews with the women as a way to underscore or further illustrate the results.

Study Design

Again, we use data from the IFS, this time on 1,225 participants who, between 1998 and 2000, were current or recent TANF recipients. About one-half were working at the time of the survey. Approximately 42 percent of the sample lacked a high school diploma or a GED, 38 percent had little work experience, and 35 percent had few job skills.[2] Approximately 22 percent of our sample reported being in poor health, and nearly 15 percent reported having a child with health problems. (We considered poor health—of a respondent or of a respondent's child—as a potential barrier to employment.) We found that approximately 6 percent reported experiencing severe domestic violence in the past year, which research also shows to impede work. Respondents were considered to have experienced domestic violence if they were subjected to at least one of six kinds of severe domestic abuse in the past year. Finally, we found that a majority of the study population were long-term welfare recipients. Approximately 42 percent received assistance for five to eight years, and another 29 percent received assistance for more than eight years between 1989 and 1998.

To assess whether the respondents were suffering from depressive symptoms, we used an abbreviated version of the Center for Epidemiological Studies Depression Scale (CES-D) (Ross, Mirowsky, & Huber, 1983). The scale registered responses to a series of questions related to mood and functioning. For example, a respondent might be asked to gauge, on a scale of 1 to 4, whether she felt that "everything I did was an effort" or "I couldn't shake the blues, even with help from family and friends." This scale measures symptoms of depression and does not provide a clinical diagnosis, but in this chapter we will use "depression," "depressive symptoms," and "symptoms of depression" interchangeably.

On the basis of this scale, 23 percent of respondents were classified as having depressive symptoms ranging from mild to severe (see table 6.1). (The classification follows the method outlined by Devins & Orme, 1984.) This falls in line with the findings of Danziger and colleagues in Michigan (2000). Most respondents reported either moderate or severe depressive symptoms—levels of depression that are more likely to impede work. Among the women we interviewed in depth, the seven in the Disaffected category were much more likely than the others to report depressive symptoms; in fact, all but two reported such symptoms. Of the twenty-seven Strivers, only five reported depressive symptoms, and only two of the twenty-four Nurturers reported depressive symptoms. Depressive symptoms among the Disaffected tend to extend for longer periods than among Strivers and Nurturers.

Tiffney, in the Disaffected category, reveals the strains of depression:

> My mother was diagnosed with terminal cancer last fall, and me and my sister took a leave of absence to take care of her. She passed away a month later. I never went back to work. I don't feel well mentally and psychologically. It's just a depression. I spend 90 percent of the time at home now. I know I can't work those hours. If I don't go back to work then, I will lose my job. I'll probably go back, but the hours are just too much and it's not flexible.

As Dionne, a woman who falls in the Disaffected category, reveals:

> I've been on disability leave since April because of depression. I've been just under so much stress with things piling up! Every time I turn around, the school wants money for some activity, my son wants money for this or that, I gotta pay for haircuts and all kinds of things. I was just working to pay bills and not enjoying it. I just had to take a break. And my job is so strict that you have to make at least 80 calls a day. I was down to only 40 calls and I was snapping on people. I snap when I'm stressed and I don't want to have to be like that.

Whereas Tiffney appears in the throes of depression, unable to quite fathom working, Diane, a Striver, has come full circle:

TABLE 6.1—Portion of IFS Sample Suffering Depressive Symptoms

Symptoms	Percentage
No symptoms	77.4
Any depressive symptoms	23.6
Mild depression	4.5
Moderate depression	9.9
Severe depression	8.2

TABLE 6.2—Mental Health Service Use (as measured by Medicaid-paid services) among Illinois' Current and Former TANF Recipients

Depression	Received Outpatient Services Hospitalization	Inpatient Psychiatric
No symptoms	5.7%	1%
Mild depression	7.3%	0%
Moderate depression	13.8%	0%
Severe depression	12.6%	1%
Total population	7.2%	1%

> I love my work very much; I make good money and I'm looking forward to my promotion. It was not always like this. I used to work five days a week and I was always exhausted. I started to become depressed. I'd sleep 15 hours a day, eat five times a day, and I started to gain weight. . . . I left the father of my children three months ago. He was part of my depression. When I started working, he stopped supporting the family financially. He thought, maybe, that since I started to work, I was able to do all the work. We stopped talking. . . . We were in this situation for one year until I got fed up, so I left him. I feel bad 'cause it affected the kids. But the situation as it was, was also affecting them bad. When I left him, I felt relieved. I was fat, eating a lot and sleeping too much. Now, I'm not depressed anymore. I lost 22 pounds.

Although we found a high level of depression among the women interviewed, in the larger study the use of mental health services was quite low. Only 8 percent of those reporting depressive symptoms in the full IFS sample received any kind of mental health treatment during the period examined. Those with moderate and severe depression were much more likely to receive services than those with mild depressive symptoms (see table 6.2). The vast majority of services were provided in outpatient settings.[3]

One reason for the low use of mental health services may be the lack of training in identification and referral among welfare caseworkers. Derr and her colleagues (2000) report that among the four states they examined, only one state had developed a standardized screening tool for identifying clients in need of such services.

Although the depressed group is demographically similar to the full study population, it is considerably more disadvantaged. About the same proportion of the depressed subsample as of the full study population lived in Cook County, was African American, and had a young child. The depressed subsample was slightly older (60% were over age thirty, compared with 55% in the full study population) and had spent a longer time receiving cash assistance before being sampled than did the full study population. More than one-third of the depressed subsample received assistance for more than eight years, compared with 29 percent of the full study population. Approximately 35 percent of the depressed subsample reported working for pay at the time of the survey, compared with just over half of the full study population. In terms of human capital, the depressed study population was more likely to have few job skills and little work experience. Almost 53 percent of this group lacked a high school diploma or GED, compared with 42 percent of the full study population. The prevalence of other health- or family-related barriers was also higher in the depressed group. Almost twice as many in the depressed subsample reported experiencing severe domestic violence in the past year (12% compared with 6%) and being in poor health (43% compared with 22%). Nearly one-fourth reported having a child in poor health, compared with 15 percent in the full study population. Although the level of mental health service use is higher among the depressed subsample, it is still low (14% compared to 8%).

Depression, Employment, Welfare, and Mental Health Services Use

What is it that distinguishes those with depressive symptoms who work, from those who have depressive symptoms and do not work? To answer that question and isolate the independent effects of depression on employment, we used a multivariate statistical method. The analysis allowed us to determine how a variety of personal characteristics (for example, education, current residence, race-ethnicity, work experience, health, presence of young children under age three, and domestic violence, among others) influence labor force participation for those with depressive symptoms. The method allowed us to view depression's singular effect on employment by holding constant the many other factors that can also influence employment.[4] Measuring outpatient claims for Medicaid mental health services, we also assessed whether having human capital has more of an effect on employment than receiving mental health services.

table 6.3 shows employment, earnings, and the duration of welfare receipt by the degree of depressive symptoms. As expected, those with symptoms of depression are less likely to be working (43% less likely than nondepressed recipients), earn less, and spend more time on welfare than the group with no depressive symptoms. Although the groups with moderate to severe depressive symptoms in particular have less employment and lower earnings than the other two groups (with none to mild symptoms), more than one-third of depressed respondents reported working at the time of the survey. This finding suggests that a substantial number of the mentally ill do work.

What allows these depressed people, who are a fairly large group, to work? We find that among those who were depressed, certain demographic and personal characteristics increased the odds of working. Race-ethnicity appears to matter. Hispanics suffering from depression, for example, were almost eight times more likely to be working than African Americans. Younger respondents (ages 20–24) were significantly less likely to be working than older respondents (age 30+). Living in a major urban area lowered the odds of working. Respondents who live in Cook County were significantly less likely to be employed than those who lived downstate in the more rural, or smaller urban, areas.

Perhaps not surprisingly, we also found that among those with moderate and severe depressive symptoms, those with "better" human capital are more likely to be working. Age, health status, job skills, and work experience are significantly associated with employment. Among those who were suffering depression, those with few job skills, for example, were 66 percent less likely to be employed than those with some job skills. Depressed respondents with little work experience were 63 percent less likely to be working than those with some experience. Interestingly, a history of domestic violence had little effect on working. Poor physical health appears to compound problems that prevent work, given that those suffering depression as well as poor health were two-thirds less likely to be working than those in good

TABLE 6.3—Depression, Employment, and Welfare among Illinois's Current and Former TANF Recipients.

Depression	Percent working at time of survey	Among those working, average earnings in the fourth quarter of 1999*	Average no. of months on AFDC/TANF since 1989
No symptoms	54.9	$3,319.61	77
Mild depression	48.4	3,307.98	80
Moderate depression	35.2	2,957.65	86
Severe depression	34.2	2,959.01	83
Total population	50.7	3,273.40	79

*Includes only those who reported working at the time of survey and had earnings reported in 1999 Q4 state unemployment insurance data. Unemployment insurance wage report records were linked to 498 respondents out of the 710 respondents who reported working at the time of survey.

health. In short, while depression impedes work, it impedes it more for those lacking personal resources that help them in the job market.

Personal Insights on Work and Depression

The meanings different people give to their depression in the context of work is interesting. To maintain their lives when dealing with depression or other health problems, some women who participated in our in-depth interviews use their children as a "reason to keep going," whereas others find it difficult to focus on their children when they are depressed. Moralisia, a Striver, had suffered profound depression and as a result had stopped talking and attempted suicide. She regained her interest in life after the birth of her child. As she explained, "I was in counseling, and that helped, but it was the birth of my daughter, going through labor, that really made the difference."

In contrast, Shaunelle, in the Disaffected group, was no longer working or attending school because of the depression that set in after her sister's death. Unable to wake up in the morning and feeling incapacitated, she spent her days at home with her children, even though they were suffering the consequences in lost school attendance. "It's not their fault. It's mine. It's harder and harder to get up in the morning to take them to school. I'm trying to stay alive to take care of my kids. . . . I think about death a lot more than I used to."

Our qualitative interviews produced dual messages about the role of work in the women's depression. Some of the Strivers found refuge in work, while others, like Tiffney, found work to be almost beyond her ability at the moment. Still others described work situations that they linked directly to their depression—too much stress, too little pay, too little control, and so forth. This raises the question of whether work contributes to, or alleviates, depression. In mental health research, work is widely recognized as important to mental health and is often a component of treatment. Work provides psychological, economic, and attitudinal benefits (Cunningham, Wolbert, & Brickmeier, 2000). Work can also provide a distraction and offer needed structure and options for socializing (Van Dongen, 1996). In fact, many individuals with mental illness both want to and do work. That said, although several studies have examined the role of mental illness in work histories, few have unraveled the direction of cause and effect. Tweed (1993), in fact, suggests that depression may have lingering effects over time, and that these effects may become an integral part of functioning, further blurring the boundaries between cause and effect (for example, work reducing depression or depression reducing work).

Regardless of whether depression affects work or work affects depression, it is perhaps more informative to look at the individual and her situation when designing policies and programs to help women achieve self-sufficiency. Dionne in the above example reveals an inability to cope and a sense of feeling overwhelmed by life, as many in the Disaffected category do. Dionne is holding a job, but it's a tenuous hold. Currently on a disability leave due to depression, she is overwhelmed by life demands that others take in stride. Strivers, for example, tend not to be as dramatically shaken the way the Disaffected are. Even if the symptoms of depression (or other health conditions, for that matter) sometimes prevent them from working, they typically continue to work and deal with their problems. They find meaning to keep them going in outward conditions or in their children. As Rashelle, a Striver, says, "I have to tell you, my strength has been my daughter. I refuse to get so down that I can't get up to feed her or walk her to school. She's the reason I started working again."

Nurturers, on the other hand, tend to be more preoccupied with the health of others, particularly their children but also other family members. Work tends to impinge on what they see as the prime role in their lives, caring for others. Yajaira, twenty-one years old with a high school degree, shares a house with her aunt and has a child with asthma. To care for her son, Yajaira has quit her job and is now "employed" as a babysitter for her aunt. "I haven't told the welfare office that my aunt just lost her job because they might make me go out and find another job. I'm not about to go out and find a job. I have to stay home with my son because he's sick. I just prefer to be able to be with my son and daughter all day."

The Strong Role (Again) of Human Capital

As our findings reveal, there appears to be a critical role for human capital that distinguishes depressed individuals who work from those who do not. In fact, in our study those who work were advantaged more by their personal skills and education and not as much by clinical help for depression. Contrary to our expectations, we found no significant effects of mental health service use. Women who used mental health services were no more likely to find jobs than women who did not. This is not entirely surprising, however, given the low rate of use of mental health services in our sample. Service use does not come easily to many poor women, and the quality and quantity of service available leaves a great deal to be desired. We also found no significant effects of having a young child, time on welfare, domestic violence, having a child in poor health, or education. This finding suggests that the usual predictors of welfare dependency were not predictive of work, and that depression was having an independent effect on work.

Taken together with the findings related to human capital in Chapter 5, the ineffectiveness of mental health services in the employment connection could suggest that job training, rather than mental health treatment, might be more effective in facilitating employment. However, as we have said earlier, we must be cautious in interpreting these results, because mental health service use in our study was quite low. Earlier research on service use among the poor suggests that we should not be particularly sanguine about effectiveness because services are poorly integrated and haphazardly used (Lewis et al., 1991). Derr and colleagues (2000) suggest that current and former TANF recipients may face a number of challenges in accessing mental health treatment. First, people who lack health insurance may find services inaccessible because of the cost. Second, the lack of culturally competent services may affect racial and ethnic minorities' access to and use of services. The Surgeon General's report on mental health among racial and ethnic minority groups (2001) notes that there are few African American and few bilingual providers of mental health services. Finally, in rural areas, the dearth of service options and the profound social stigma surrounding mental illness are likely to impede service for residents. One or more of these factors, or others, might contribute to the low rates of mental health service use found in this study.[5]

The success of welfare reform is shaped by what the person brings to the situation. Depression can impede work, but, as our results show, it does not always or necessarily do so. Many of our depressed respondents were working, and some found work to be a welcome diversion. For others, depression cast a pall over their world, zapping their desire to work—or to do much else for that matter.

CHAPTER 7

How the Children Fare

LIBERALS AND CONSERVATIVES in the United States didn't agree on much when it came to welfare reform—except that any changes should help improve the lives of the children of welfare recipients. Of course, how to do that was a major bone of contention. As we described in chapter 1, in the minds of liberals, PRWORA diminished the life chances of poor children, and in the view of conservatives, it improved the children's situation. The two camps forecast very different outcomes if poor mothers were required to leave welfare and go to work. Liberals predicted that families would have less income and would decline; conservatives believed that families would have more income and better opportunities as recipients were spurred into the labor market.

Neither camp intended to hurt the children of the very poor, but if their theories were flawed, the children might very well suffer. While neither side was sanguine about AFDC, liberals believed that welfare served as a safety net (although a tattered one) that kept poor children fed and clothed in the worst of conditions. Leaving mothers to fend for themselves in the labor market without increased skills or economic support was seen as a recipe for disaster. Fewer resources meant more stress for the family and most likely poorer performance by children in school and in life, liberals contended. Educational outcomes were the most important among many outcomes that would affect children adversely.

Conservatives predicted a more positive outcome of the reform. Shorn of the dependency and pathologies of the dole, women, they contended, would find work and improve their mental health (and in doing so, become better mothers). The result should be an improvement in educational outcomes for the children. The key to the debate between right and left was the effect of a mother's work on the lives of her offspring. Would poor mothers find work, and would that work have a positive effect on educational (and other important) outcomes?

In this chapter we look to see which predictions come closer to the truth. To examine the question of how the children are doing, we return to our larger sample of one thousand women, all of whom are poor mothers who were on welfare at the beginning of the study.

The effect of a mother's work on children has a long research history, and much of the debate is politically charged. The debate often centers on children with two parents, with one side arguing that having a mother who works does no harm (assuming high-quality child care is available), and the other arguing that it leads to poorer outcomes for children and society. Interestingly, debaters often switch sides when applying the argument to welfare mothers. Conservatives, who often argue that mothers of young children should not work, argue that welfare mothers must work, while some liberals find themselves arguing that mothers should stay home with their children. When the PRWORA debate emerged in the early 1990s, liberals found themselves arguing against "forced" work while conservatives found themselves supporting work for mothers who had been on welfare.

The research on whether it is good or bad for children when low-income (often single) mothers work is mixed. Although research has shown that maternal employment can have positive—or at least not negative—effects on school outcomes for children of low-income mothers (Huston et al., 2001; Smith et al., 2003; Moore & Driscoll, 1997; Morris et al., 2001; Zaslow & Emig, 1997), much depends on the particular situation. Women entering the workforce from welfare often take menial jobs for low pay, which can have a strong influence on children's outcomes. Children whose mothers earn higher wages (Moore & Driscoll, 1997) and work in less menial and more mentally demanding jobs (Menaghan & Parcel, 1995; Parcel & Menaghan, 1997) appear to do better than their counterparts. Further, welfare receipt itself, especially when it is not coupled with work, has been shown to have negative effects on children's outcomes (Smith et al., 2000; Lohman et al., 2004). On the other hand, when a parent does not find a job but is forced to leave welfare, the loss of income can have serious detrimental effects on children. Many studies have shown that living in poverty is associated with negative cognitive and academic outcomes for children (for example, Collins & Aber, 1997; Duncan et al., 1998; Guo, 1998; Brooks-Gunn & Duncan, 1997).

There is a variety of factors that shape the effect of mothers' employment. The gender of the child matters. Boys appear to benefit more than girls from their mothers' employment (Huston et al., 2001). One study found children whose mothers were consistently employed or consistently unemployed over a time span did better in school than those whose mothers entered and left the workforce frequently, indicating that job stability may be important (Secret & Peck-Heath, 2004). In addition, the timing of a mother's employment matters. Elementary school children in families receiving welfare appeared to do better when their mothers worked, while teens fared worse in school. Teens also had more behavior problems and minor delinquent activity (Morris et al., 2001; Duncan & Chase-Lansdale, 2001). In addition, some research has found more behavior problems in subsequent years when mothers work more hours during children's early years (Parcel & Menaghan, 1994). In an important article, Chase-Lansdale and her colleagues found no substantial negative impact of welfare reform on children, but neither did they find much positive effect (Chase-Lansdale et al., 2003).

Work requirements may also limit the time parents can spend helping their children with schoolwork, reading to them, and further exposing them to the things that boost their school performance. Several of the mothers in our study spoke about the time they spent preparing their children for school. A typical day for Madelyn, for example, involves assisting her sons with their after-school homework, which, she says, "usually takes about an hour." She has enrolled them in karate classes at the park district two nights a week. She also frequently takes her children to the library, where they check out "stacks and stacks of books." The library offers free reading programs as well.

Mattie, whose daughter is a straight A student and whose son is an A/B student, walks her children to the bus every day. After school the children go to a community youth center. "At the center the teachers help the kids with homework, and the kids get to play on computers. The kids have friends there, and the teachers are nice and take them on field trips." Mattie pays $5 per child for the school year, but her children do not go to the community center during the summer because it costs $100 per child.

A mother's involvement with her children has been shown to be important to academic achievement (Henderson & Berla, 1994; Epstein, 2001; Hoover-Dempsey & Sandler, 1995; Steinberg, 1996; Zellman & Waterman, 1998; Bogenschneider, 1997; Izzo et al., 1999). At least part of the positive effect stems from parents initiating and sharing in school-related activities in the home (SuiChu & Willms, 1996). For a single mother, balancing work and family life can be difficult (Edin & Lein, 1997). The welfare law requires recipients to work at least thirty hours per week (proposals under PROWRA reauthorization boost the work requirement even higher), leaving less time to be actively involved in children's schooling. Nurturers especially find this work requirement onerous. As Sheila, a mother of three who falls into our Nurturer category, said, "It's traumatic for mothers to be taken from their kids. It's not that I don't want to work, but my kids don't know nobody but me, and it's like I was taken from my kids. I don't go to their parent conferences and plays, but when I wasn't working, I would go to those things."

Strivers, in contrast, often find ways to balance work and family by seeking work with night shifts so they can be at home after school or by making child-care arrangements. Melody, a 29-year-old Striver and mother of two, works full-time and proudly reports that she never misses work unless her daughter is sick. She has found a schedule that can accommodate her children by working the first shift from 7 a.m. to 3 p.m. "so I will be able to be with them."

However, as some have proposed, child care may be a more stimulating environment academically for certain children, mainly those whose parents are less involved in schooling or whose home life might be chaotic and unstructured. For those youngsters, getting out of the home for some structured time in day care—if it is high-quality and affordable—may be beneficial.

These findings can be frustrating for policy makers because they offer no clear-cut direction for policy changes. Boys seem to do better than girls when their mothers work, but not if their mothers work too many hours, and not if the boys are in their teens. Girls seem to persevere in school regardless of their mothers' workload. Mothers, however, might be better parents if they worked less—or not, depending on the mother. And therein lies the key: depending on the mother. Employment matters, depending on the person and the situation.

The Current Study

To assess whether a mother's employment since welfare reform has affected her children, we examine children's academic performance as measured by test scores, a key indicator of future success. We assess outcomes for 984 children from the full IFS sample. We monitor their progress from 1999, when welfare reform was in its early years, to 2003, when mothers had had ample time in the workforce. The majority of the children, 73 percent, attended Chicago Public Schools, while the remaining one-fourth were schooled outside of Cook County. In 1999, 20 percent of the children were doing poorly in school (earning grades below C), and 17 percent had changed schools in the last year, a sign of families in flux, which can be detrimental to children. Ten percent were in poor health, and 14 percent had missed at least one week of school. Just over 10 percent had a behavioral disorder.

To gauge academic achievement, we rely on results from standardized tests—in this case the Iowa Test of Basic Skills. The scores, measured as percentile rank, indicate math and reading ability. We assessed differences in these scores depending on mothers' work histories. Mothers were considered working if they earned $650 or more during each of the thirty quarters analyzed, and not working if they earned less. (To earn $650 during a quarter, a woman working for $5 an hour would have had to work ten hours a week.) We also parsed the results for those whose time in the workforce had increased by at least 25 percent between the first and the last interviews; those whose work had increased more than 25 percent; those whose time in the workforce had decreased; and those whose workload stayed the same.

We used a regression analysis to estimate the likelihood over time of improved standardized test scores as measured by the Iowa tests. As in prior chapters, we controlled for factors that might influence outcomes—in this case, race-ethnicity, gender, age, health, previous grades, special education, absenteeism, school change, amount of time parents spent with children on homework (more or less than two hours a week), and externalizing behavior problems, as measured by the Externalizing Problems from the Social Skills Rating System. We also controlled for maternal characteristics that are associated with children's outcomes, including age, marital status, health, high school diploma or GED, being held back in a grade, and symptoms of depression. Since the neighborhood can also affect school outcomes, we included controls for that as well. These included living in the city, the number of children, a family's current welfare receipt, if the family was a long-term welfare recipient, income, social support, other financial support, parenting stress, parenting warmth, discipline, neighborhood safety and satisfaction, and hardship or housing problems. Finally, the conditions in the school obviously can affect outcomes. We controlled for student-teacher ratio, minority concentration, limited English proficiency rate, mobility rate, the number of teachers with emergency credentials, and overall test performance.

Boys Affected More than Girls by Their Mothers' Workforce Participation

Test scores reveal how the rate of children's growth varies over time based on their personal characteristics. That is, we estimate each child's math and reading test score change over time and calculate how this growth varies between children based on changes in parental work and other child-specific characteristics. This tells us which children's test scores increase at a faster rate over time. Although Child A may have lower scores in 2003, she may have seen faster growth over the four-year period than another child whose grades were actually higher in 2003. Point-in-time studies will miss this important nuance.

Looking at rate of growth, we found that among boys whose mothers significantly increased their work hours (more than a 26% increase) between 1999 and 2003, math scores declined and reading scores increased at a slower pace than those of their peers whose parent worked only slightly more or who worked less over the time period. That is, their math scores on standardized tests declined more than did those of their peers whose mothers worked only slightly more (1% to 25% more) over time or not at all. In this case, moderate to large increases in mothers' work negatively affected boys' math scores and appeared to slow their progress in reading. Given the current climate of high-stakes testing, it is worrisome if boys' test scores decline as mothers increase their workload. Girls were not significantly affected by their mother's work schedule.

We also found that academic achievement decreased with age and special education placement and that children whose parents had ever been retained in a grade were significantly less likely to receive high grades than were children whose parents had not been held back. Parents who struggled in school are perhaps less likely to be able to provide academic support for their children (Lareau, 1989). Children whose parents reported symptoms of depression were also less likely to achieve academically than were those whose parents were not depressed—not surprising, given that maternal depression has been linked to adverse outcomes in infants and young children (Petterson & Albers, 2001).

Contrary to previous research (Amato, 2001), we found that children of divorced or separated parents were significantly more likely to get good grades than were their peers whose parents had never been married.

We also found that the strongest predictors of academic achievement were children's prior grades. A special education placement was a strong indicator of poor grades. Both findings are not surprising but again underscore the importance of human capital. Those families with higher cognitive abilities would have that reflected in these educational outcomes. Surprisingly, when parents helped with homework, children's grades and test scores declined. It could be that parents who become involved with homework are doing so because their children are already struggling. Interestingly, we find no relationship between school characteristics and children's academic achievement, suggesting that there may be more intra-school variation than inter-school variation. Of course, the majority of children in the study were attending high-poverty, largely segregated schools, so we may have been unable to capture the influence of school conditions in our sample.

There are several reasons why some degree of parental work may boost academic achievement, at least temporarily. Especially among families that receive work supports, parental employment could provide the child with more stability, a daily routine, and a positive parental role model. Employment could also lead to improved psychological well-being for the parent, which could lead to better parenting and improved outcomes for the child (Huston et al., 2001; Zaslow et al., 2002).

Finally, and also surprisingly, high neighborhood satisfaction was correlated with declining math scores. As we show in future chapters, this may be because respondents who are more satisfied with their neighborhoods (regardless of its conditions) were less likely to move to a better neighborhood. While our results on the relationship between work and the child's educational achievement are complicated, they do show that work is in and of itself neither a curse nor a panacea. Given the overall success of PRWORA, we should look more closely at the factors that shape how work affects the educational achievement of children, for work will be an important part of the policy menu for many years to come.

SECTION 3

Policy Factors Influencing

the Poor in Illinois

CHAPTER 8

Sanctions

Do They Help or Hurt the Poor?

AS DESCRIBED IN CHAPTER 1, the conservative Charles Murray argued in the prelude to welfare reform that the current system created a disincentive to work. In a country that values work and the self-made individual, he said, welfare was limiting the opportunities for thousands of poor mothers and families. In Murray's argument, welfare was set up in such a way as to encourage mothers not to marry and to have additional children in order to get bigger welfare checks. Recipients were therefore acting rationally by staying on welfare and not working. Taking this argument to heart, welfare reforms built in not only a mandate to work in exchange for welfare but also various carrots and sticks to prod women into the workforce and off welfare. A key device was the sanction—the reduction or elimination of the welfare check for noncompliance with rules.

Sanctions of one form or another have long been used to regulate the behavior of welfare recipients (Handler & Hasenfeld, 1991), but the extent of sanctioning was usually limited to the caregiver's portion of the AFDC grant, so that the child would not be punished by the rule violations of the adult (Pavetti, Derr, & Hesketh, 2003). Sanctions play an integral role under current TANF policies and can result in the loss of the entire welfare grant. Indeed, sanctions form the basis of a new social contract with welfare recipients: work is expected in exchange for temporary monetary and in-kind assistance (Pavetti & Wemmerus, 1999). Supporters of this approach argue that the combination of carrots and sticks makes work the preferred, or rational, option, and that the declines in welfare caseloads are evidence that these devices work.

Critics argue that the majority of welfare recipients want to work, and that when provided not with sanctions but with the right incentives (for example, earned income disregards, living-wage jobs, etc.) will choose employment over welfare. Sanctions, they argue, may push people into low-wage jobs that fail to provide adequate support for their families. Under this scenario, sanctions may have a more punitive effect and could cause further hardship for families already living on low incomes.

States vary in their sanction policies. Some states, such as California, quickly impose full sanctions for failure to work, while others allow more leniency. Illinois's policy finds the middle ground between sticks and carrots. On the one hand, Illinois offers several work supports that in theory should make work pay more than welfare. On the other hand, it imposes a series of progressively stiffer sanctions for not working. A first instance of noncompliance leads to cash benefits being cut in half until the recipient cooperates. "Noncompliance" could mean a missed meeting with the caseworker, failure to file necessary paperwork or work or income report forms, refusal to work, failure to show up for required job preparation courses if not working, or, if a minor, failure to attend school or GED classes. Recipients may also be sanctioned for failure to cooperate with child support enforcement, failure to have a child immunized, or failure to ensure the child attends school. A second infraction is followed by a three-month loss of half of one's benefits. The most serious sanction is a full loss of welfare benefits for three months after three instances of noncompliance.

Between 1999 and June 2003, 36 percent of the respondents in our Illinois Families Study had experienced a partial or full sanction. Eighty percent had their TANF cases closed at least once between 1999 and 2001, although not all of these were because of sanctions. For example, some recipients married or had earnings above the eligibility rules. Distinctions between people receiving sanctions become more apparent over time. Among respondents receiving TANF in 1999, 13 percent were sanctioned, compared with 23 percent of those receiving TANF in 2000, in 2001, and in 2002. However, by 2003, this share would drop dramatically, to only 6 percent, although information on sanctions was only available through June of that year. Often, one sanction was enough. The majority of respondents who received a first-level sanction received no more. On average, sanctioned respondents were more likely to have participated in a job search or job training program, to have a child with an adverse health condition, and to have slightly more children under age 18. They were also less likely to be working or married and more likely to be aware of the earnings disregard policy (see table 8.1).

As noted, proponents argue that sanctions create incentives to follow the rules and find a job—that they are a necessary prod for some. Indeed, early studies of states with more strident sanction policies found higher rates of welfare-to-work exits (Hofferth, Stanhope, & Harris, 2000), and states with immediate full sanctions had greater caseload declines than states with more

TABLE 8.1—Characteristics of Respondents Who Experienced Partial or Full Sanctions

Selected Characteristics as of 2003	1999–2003 No Sanction	Sanction
Rent is government subsidized	36%	39%
Currently working*	54%	25%
Participated in job search/job training program*	9%	22%
Ave. cumulative months receiving AFDC/TANF prior to 1999	79	83
Married*	13%	7%
Ave. age of youngest child	6.5	6.0
Any children with health conditions limiting their activities*	15%	24%
Number of children under age 18*	2.5	2.8
Chronic health problems	34%	38%
High school degree or GED	51%	45%
Unaware of earnings disregards*	47%	38%

Analyses are restricted to the 823 respondents in 2003 who consented to administrative data access and who received TANF at some point between 1999 and June 2003.

* $p < 0.05$, chi-square tests

Source: IFS survey data and Illinois Dept. of Human Services administrative data. *The Two Worlds of Welfare Reform in Illinois: Fourth Annual Report.* Evanston, IL: University Consortium on Welfare Reform, July 2004.

lenient policies (Rector & Youssef, 1999). These earlier studies did not attempt to link these caseload declines to the level of disadvantage the sanctioned might experience. However, a large study by researchers at Mathematica, which specializes in evaluating various welfare and workforce programs, found that those who are sanctioned are typically more disadvantaged (Pavetti, Derr, & Hesketh, 2003). Others have arrived at similar conclusions (Kalil et al., 2002; Cherlin et al., 2002; Shook, 1999). Those sanctioned often had less education, more children, poorer health, and more disruptive life events, such as frequent moving, threats of eviction, and so forth. Our own results concur. IFS respondents who had partial or full sanctions experienced, on average, more hardship than those not sanctioned, and they were significantly more likely to experience utility shutoffs (see table 8.2). They were also more likely to reduce expenses by moving in with others.

To further explore who is sanctioned and why, we examine how welfare sanctions affect employment, earnings, hardship, and welfare use among 1,123 participants in the Illinois Families Study between January 1999 and March 2001. For analyses related to hardship, we rely on the 921 people who participated in all three interviews of the study, since our hardship measures were not assessed until the final interview in the study. We asked respondents about their ability to pay rent, whether they had had their gas or electricity turned off since the last interview, and whether they sometimes had gone without food or did not have enough to eat.

Study Design

To examine sanctioning effects, we relied on administrative data tracking employment earnings (reported in the Illinois Unemployment Insurance system) and the welfare agency's records of sanction, case closures, and welfare exit. We also gauged the effect of the threat of sanction versus actual sanctions. If sanctions induce changes in behavior, we should see no different effect between actual sanctions and the threat of sanctions. If sanctions are more of a punitive tool, however, then we should see greater hardship among those sanctioned than among those merely threatened with a sanction. Finally, to better isolate the effect of a sanction, we also include the effect of reductions in the welfare grant for other reasons, such as an increase in earnings, changes in the number of eligible children at home, marriage, or worker error. This allows us to distinguish whether these other types of grant loss are functionally similar to sanctions in their effect on families. It is also possible that recipients may change their behavior in response to simply knowing about the sanction policy. We therefore asked recipients about their knowledge of a set of welfare rules (time limits, earnings disregards, etc.), and ranked their understanding on a scale of 1–5.

We employed both bivariate and multivariate analyses to predict the effects on welfare, work, earnings, and hardship, controlling for other potentially confounding factors such as previous involvement with work, learning disability, English language fluency, job skills, chronic health conditions, domestic violence in the last year, depression, substance abuse, and lack of a car or a driver's license. We also controlled for certain demographic characteristics (age, number of children, race-ethnicity, family structure), attitudes toward welfare and other welfare experiences, knowledge of welfare rules, social support, and a set of neighborhood factors measuring social capital (such as safety of neighborhood, and neighbors who help one another). Before we discuss the results of these analyses, we provide a snapshot of who experienced sanctions.

TABLE 8.2–Sanctions and Material Hardship

Selected Characteristics as of 2003	No Sanction	Sanction
Phone service turned off*	25%	33%
Gas/electricity turned off*	7%	11%
Evicted	3%	4%
Respondent or child needed to see doctor but could not afford to go	9%	7%
Respondent or child could not afford to fill a prescription	8%	5%
Moved in with others to reduce expenses*	5%	9%
Can generally afford to buy things they need	65%	60%
Sought help from charity or church for clothes or financial aid	8%	8%
Worried children did not have enough to eat	6%	7%
Homeless	3%	3%
Lived in two or more places since last interview	25%	24%

Analyses are restricted to the 823 respondents in 2003 who consented to administrative data access and who received TANF at some point between 1999 and June 2003

* $p < 0.05$, chi-square tests

Source: IFS survey data and Illinois Dept. of Human Services administrative data.

Who Gets Sanctioned and Why

Among the respondents, approximately 20 percent had sanctions, and 8 percent had sanctions initiated but lifted before a grant loss (labeled as "threat to sanction"). Approximately two-thirds of the respondents had other types of grant reductions unrelated to sanctions, and almost 80 percent had their TANF cases closed at least once during the study period.

We found that, even after controlling for other factors likely to affect work, such as previous work involvement, those who experienced sanctions were about half as likely to be working as those who experienced no sanctions (see table 8.3). There appears to be more than economic rationality at work here. If welfare, as conservatives argued, created

TABLE 8.3—Predictors of Welfare, Work, and Earnings

Independent Variables	Being Off TANF Odds Ratio (SE)	Work Odds Ratio (SE)	Earnings Beta Unstandardized (SE)
Welfare Receipt and Earnings			
No. months on TANF during IFS	0.82 (.01)**	1.00 (.01)	-25.44 (15.95)
No. months on AFDC/ TANF pre-IFS	1.00 (.00)	1.00 (.00)	5.04 (3.46)
Earnings 1995–1998	1.03 -0.07	1.39 (.07)**	702.93 (86.84)**
Earnings 1999–2001	—	—	—
Sanction and Grant Loss Factors			
Sanction	.74 (.21)	.47 (.19)**	-1325.97 (254.45)**
Threat of sanction	1.22 (.30)	.73 (.27)	-57.81 (366.14)
Grant reduction	.70 (.20)+	1.52 (.16)**	-14.61 (219.38)
Case terminated	—	.76 (.22)	27.46 (297.16)
Sum of knowledge of welfare rules	1.17 (.07)*	1.21 (.05)**	275.88 (74.19)**
Demographic Variables			
Age at wave 1	1.03 (.02)	.97 (.01)*	-7.75 (19.22)
Age at time of first birth	1.02 (.03)	.96 (.02)*	-46.81 (31.06)
Married, living together with spouse	3.44 (.42)**	.86 (.27)	-96.30 (369.42)
Unmarried, living together with partner	1.25 (.43)	.65 (.33)	-376.75 (452.17)
Number other workers in home	1.44 (.32)	.62 (.26)+	-1026.18 (350.18)**
Number of children in home	.95 (.07)	1.02 (.06)	51.15 (82.67)
Age of youngest child	.97 (.03)	1.03 (.02)	43.86 (31.09)
Hispanic	2.93 (.33)**	2.20 (.27)**	971.87 (361.19)**
Non-Hispanic white	2.16 (.41)+	1.60 (.30)	440.69 (408.27)
Cook County resident	.57 (.34)+	1.15 (.26)	432.38 (353.18)
Factors Affecting Employment			
High school education	1.18 (.19)	1.28 (.16)	513.14 (217.34)*
Learning disability	.65 (.38)	.92 (.32)	-854.90 (421.81)*
Trouble reading in English	1.45 (.40)	.91 (.32)	-244.08 (425.08)
Few job skills	1.38 (.19)+	.77 (.16)	122.19 (220.40)
Child with chronic health problem	.89 (.21)	.96 (.17)	-287.01 (239.14)

Severe domestic violence past year	1.40 (.40)	.48 (.35)*	-1032.37 (464.96)*
Poor health (self-rated)	3.10 (.43)**	.56 (.34)+	-230.22 (445.69)
Chronic health condition	.84 (.23) ′	.76 (.19)	-373.00 (258.03)
Depression	.78 (.22)	.66 (.19)*	-348.25 (253.54)
Frequent alcohol or drug use	1.67 (.37)	1.00 (.32)	-122.02 (440.26)
No car/driver's license	.86 (.22)	.50 (.18)**	-975.76 (243.64)**

Expectations and Experiences

Neighborhood safe	.79 (.18)	1.13 (.15)	242.96 (209.92)
Neighbors help each other	.69 (.18)*	1.21 (.15)	-280.12 (205.33)
Informal work activity	.67 (.29)	.51 (.26)**	-553.43 (343.42)
Social support	.92 (.04)*	.92 (.04)*	-80.31 (48.30)+
Subsidized housing resident	.67 (.19)*	1.32 (.16)+	-87.20 (221.11)
Formal child support	.94 (.25)	.66 (.20)*	71.21 (275.20)
Informal child support	1.29 (.19)	.97 (.15)	231.89 (206.83)
Believes in right to receive welfare	1.10 (.10)	.88 (.08)	-16.49 (112.09)
Expect to be receiving welfare in one year	.99 (.10)	1.05 (.08)	-113.12 (110.14)
Worker takes time to explain rules	1.18 (.08)*	.81 (.06)**	-210.73 (86.67)*
Family of origin received welfare	.70 (.19)+	.52 (.16)**	-490.13 (218.31)*
Missing info on family of origin	1.24 (.37)	.62 (.31)	-308.74 (426.32)
Goal orientation	1.07 (.03)*	1.08 (.02)**	56.34 (28.83)+
Number of requirements imposed by worker	.84 (.10)+	.86 (.08)+	-59.13 (111.73)
CONSTANT	2.77 (1.04)	2.38 (.90)	3715.07 (1215.71)
Percent correctly classified	88%	72%	—
Adjusted R-squared	—	—	20%

** $p < 0.01$, * $p < 0.05$, + $p < 0.10$
Note: $N = 1109$. Total sample size for the Wave 1 respondents=1123; 14 cases were omitted from analyses due to missing data. Also, additional 20 cases with extreme outliers for earnings in the outcome variable (>$15,000 in one quarter) were excluded in the earnings regression analysis.

incentives to remain on aid and not work, then threatening a cutoff of that aid for not working should induce women to work. Among our sample of women, however, this was not the case. In fact, sanctions were associated with less work. From this one might surmise that other complications and personal impediments are the reason certain women were not working. Indeed, we found other factors that lowered the likelihood of working, including age, histories of domestic violence, depression, and lack of a car or a driver's license (see table 8.3).

In contrast, threats of sanction (a sanction was initiated but lifted without grant loss) had no discernible effect on employment. A grant reduction for other reasons than sanction, however, more than doubled the odds of working. Although women might not be working, perhaps the incentive prods them to leave welfare even without a job—which conservative pundits agreed was a step in the right direction. As we reported elsewhere, nearly half of the IFS sample were neither working nor receiving welfare at the end of our study. Perhaps sanctions had involuntarily pushed them off the rolls, but we found no evidence that a sanction or a threat of a sanction induced women to leave TANF, once other factors were controlled (table 8.3). In fact, certain demographic variables are much more important in predicting a welfare exit, especially an exit into a job, than sanctions. Top among them was being married. Those who were married were more than three times as likely to have left welfare than those who were not. Other important factors were having high goal orientation, being Hispanic or white, and having caseworkers who took more time to explain program rules. On the other hand, a long history of welfare, having greater social support, and living in public housing made a recipient less likely to leave welfare. Those whose TANF grants were reduced for reasons other than sanction were 70 percent more likely to leave TANF than those without grant reductions.

If sanctions served to remove from the rolls those who could already take care of themselves without welfare, one would expect to find fairly robust earnings among this group. However, we found just the opposite. Those who were sanctioned earned, on average, about $1,320 less in the two quarters prior to the survey than those not sanctioned. As seen in past chapters, human capital remained important to higher earnings. Having a high school diploma was associated with higher earnings (see table 8.3). Also associated with higher earnings was being Hispanic. In contrast, earnings were not affected by a threat of sanction or by having one's grant reduced for other reasons.

Our analysis suggests that sanctions were not affecting work but they were creating hardships, having a particularly large effect on hardships related to food (table 8.4). Those who were sanctioned were three times more likely to report food hardship in the past several months than those not sanctioned. A grant reduction for other reasons had no effect on food hardship, but it did increase the risk of having one's utilities cut off and of facing rent hardship. The threat of sanction affected only rent hardship. Being threatened more than doubled the likelihood of rent hardship. It may be that those struggling with rent are sanctioned because their housing issues make it difficult to comply with welfare rules and work mandates. However, those with housing issues also might be more likely to be viewed sympathetically by workers and end up having the sanction removed prior to an actual grant loss.

TABLE 8.4—Predictors of Material Hardships

Independent Variables	Rent Hardship *Odds Ratio* *(S.E.)*	Utility Hardship *Odds Ratio* *(S.E.)*	Food Hardship *Odds Ratio* *(S.E.)*	Perceived Hardship *Unstandardized* *Coefficient (S.E)*
Welfare Receipt and Earnings				
No. months on TANF during IFS	1.03 (.02)	1.04 (.03)	.99 (.03)	.003 (.01)
No. months on AFDC/ TANF pre-IFS)	1.01 (.001	1.01 (.01)	1.01 (.01)*	.01 (.003)**
Earnings 1995–1998 (in $10,000s)	.98 (.08)	1.01 (.11)	1.17 (.09) +	.01 (.05)
Earnings 1999–2001 (in $10,000s)	.93 (.09)	.76 (.15) +	1.02 (.15)	-.13 (.06)*
Sanction and Grant Loss Factors				
Sanction	.95 (.27)	.51 (.39)+	3.17 (.41)**	.27 (.23)
Threat of sanction	2.27 (.36)*	.97 (.57)	1.35 (.54)	-.12 (.31)
Grant reduction	2.96 (.31)**	2.83 (.40)**	.57 (.43)	.44 (.20)*
Case terminated	.81 (.31)	.90 (.43)	.43 (.46) +	.36 (.25)
Sum of knowledge of welfare rules	.93 (.08)	1.21 (.12)	.75 (.12)*	-.04 (.06)
Demographic Information				
Age at Wave 1	1.01 (.02)	1.07 (.03)*	1.01 (.03)	-.01 (.02)
Age at time of first birth	1.00 (.03)	1.06 (.04)	1.00 (.05)	.03 (.03)
Married, living with spouse	1.19 (.44)	6.87 (.45)**	2.65 (.59) +	.42 (.32)
Unmarried, living together	2.07 (.48)	.51 (.79)	.20 (.95) +	-.04 (.38)
Number of other workers in home	.78 (.41)	.84 (.54)	1.72 (.57)	-.68 (.29)*
Number of children in home	.92 (.09)	.83 (.13)	.67 (.16)*	.001 (.07)
Age of youngest child	.99 (.04)	.97 (.05)	.94 (.05)	-.04 (.03)
Hispanic	.68 (.43)	3.58 (.44)**	1.14 (.59)	-.76 (.30)*
Non-Hispanic white	1.38 (.42)	.50 (.62)	1.93 (.70)	-.36 (.36)
Cook County resident	1.71 (.40)	.88 (.50)	.80 (.66)	1.13 (.30)**
Factors Affecting Employment				
High school education	1.38 (.25)	.68 (.32)	1.28 (.37)	-.29 (.19)
Learning disability	.19 (.68)*	.73 (.60)	1.13 (.65)	.98 (.34)**
Trouble reading in English	.42 (.55)	.02 (1.38)**	.57 (.92)	-.15 (.36)
Few job skills	1.45 (.24)	1.19 (.32)	.66 (.36)	-.80 (.19)**
Child with chronic health problem	.96 (.26)	.93 (.35)	.97 (.42)	-.67 (.20)**

Severe domestic violence past year	1.04 (.43)	.70 (.65)	.26 (.79) +	.01 (.37)
Poor health (self-rated)	.57 (.49)	2.47 (.54) +	2.12 (.57)	.05 (.37)
Chronic health condition	1.19 (.29)	1.23 (.38)	.77 (.46)	-.09 (.22)
Depression	1.49 (.26)	.89 (.37)	.85 (.40)	.07 (.22)
Frequent alcohol or drug use	.92 (.47)	1.22 (.68)	12.81 (.53)**	-.67 (.39) +
No car/driver's license	.45 (.28)**	.36 (.37)**	5.33 (.62)**	-.06 (.21)

Experiences and Expectations

Neighborhood safe	1.02 (.24)	.96 (.33)	1.78 (.39)	.40 (.18)*
Neighbors help each other	.95 (.23)	1.49 (.32)	.64 (.35)	-.01 (.17)
Informal work activity	1.77 (.33)+	2.54 (.45)*	.91 (.59)	.06 (.29)
Social support	.91 (.05)+	.95 (.07)	.80 (.07)**	-.14 (.04)**
Subsidized housing resident	.49 (.26)**	.86 (.33)	1.05 (.37)	-.09 (.19)
Formal child support	.85 (.30)	1.77 (.38)	1.28 (.48)	-.56 (.23)*
Informal child support	1.03 (.23)	.86 (.31)	.76 (.35)	.16 (.17)
Believes in right to receive welfare	1.07 (.13)	.94 (.18)	1.49 (.20)*	.14 (.09)
Expect to be receiving welfare in one year	1.14 (.12)	1.36 (.16) +	1.36 (.16) +	.17 (.09) +
Worker takes time to explain rules	.78 (.10)**	.63 (.13)**	1.09 (.15)	-.05 (.07)
Family of origin received welfare	1.10 (.25)	3.09 (.34)**	1.25 (.38)	.09 (.19)
Missing info on family of origin	1.17 (.52)	4.16 (.79) +	.06 (2.69)	-.05 (.41)
Goal orientation	.98 (.03)	1.01 (.04)	.88 (.05)*	-.06 (.03)*
Number of requirements imposed by worker	.81 (.13)+	1.11 (.18)	1.008 (.21)	.12 (.10)
CONSTANT	.34 (1.35)	.002 (1.90)	.43 (2.05)	11.74 (1.05)**
Percent correctly classified	86%	92%	94%	—
Adjusted R-squared	—	—	—	0.12

** $p < 0.01$, * $p < 0.05$, + $p < 0.10$
Note: $N = 913$. Total sample size for Wave 3 respondents = 921; 8 cases were omitted from analyses due to missing data.

In summary, we found no indication that imposed sanctions are promoting work and reducing welfare dependency as intended; in fact, they are associated with less work and lower earnings. The results also suggest that the primary way that sanctions are operating is not to induce behavior changes—the odds of working actually declined, and women were no more likely to leave TANF than were those who were not sanctioned—but as a punitive measure.

The data can reveal the overall trends and correlations between sanctions and employment, earnings, and hardship, but they leave us wondering what personal factors lead to a sanction and how the women experience the sanctions. Individual circumstances are unique, and a blanket policy intended to alter behavior might resonate for certain individuals but ring hollow for others. Ultimately, policy will be more effective if we understand these differences and tailor programs and policies accordingly. We now turn, therefore, to the interview data to gain more personal insight into the experience of a sanction.

How Sanctions and Welfare Loss Look to the Person

In October 1999, Claribel, whom we would classify as a Nurturer according to our schema, received her last cash grant from welfare. She was sanctioned for not revealing a pregnancy to her caseworker. "I did report it," she said, "but later in December. They also reduced my grant because I didn't have the 20 hours of work I needed. I tried applying at a lot of places, but never got hired. All I wanted was at least Medicaid for my daughter, but they never gave it to me. They told me I was married to a man, but I'm not, and that he can support both my children since he lives here."

Among the fifty-eight women in our personal interviews, thirty-one reported that they had lost their entire cash welfare benefit or had left welfare for one or more months in the past year. Of these, nine were sanctioned, and twenty became employed or earned too much to continue to qualify. One woman was unsure why she lost benefits, and another had sought assistance from another program. Approximately equal numbers of Nurturers, Strivers, and Disaffected were sanctioned.

Lawanda, who is Disaffected, refused a job and resisted giving the caseworker information on her situation. To continue receiving $212 per month in cash welfare, Lawanda was required to contact at least ten employers a week. Without a car, and not being "a bus person," she did not consider jobs in the suburbs. She was angry with the welfare office because it had threatened to cut her benefits if she failed to give them complete information on her living arrangements or the Social Security number of the father of her child. "They made me wait three hours for an appointment and fill out the same forms over and over. They pressure me to just sign off on forms without being able to read them first and threatened me with cutting my benefits for not giving them all the information they asked for. They were rude to me." By the second interview a year later, Lawanda was no longer receiving welfare benefits. "I'm ineligible for welfare. I received a letter immediately cutting my benefits off because I had been overpaid $5,000."

While sanctions were dispersed fairly evenly, more Strivers lost their benefits because of an earnings gain or employment. Of the twenty women who reported losing their entire cash benefit in the previous year because of a job or higher earnings, eleven were Strivers, seven were Nurturers, and two were in the Disaffected category.

In addition to a full loss of their welfare check, fifteen women reported that they had experienced a partial grant reduction in the previous year. The majority of these women had lost their benefits only once in the previous year. The most common reasons for losing benefits were missing an appointment with a caseworker and failing to file paperwork. There was no strong distinction between the Strivers and Nurturers in the reasons for partial sanctions.

Janet, a member of the Disaffected group, missed an appointment with her caseworker because of other conflicts. "The job program ran until noon, and the appointment was scheduled for 2:30. I had gone home and couldn't afford to return to the welfare office for the appointment. There should have been more of an effort to coordinate the appointment with my work program schedule. I didn't know I had been sanctioned until my next monthly check was cut by half. Program requirements are only fair if a job can be guaranteed."

Dora, a Nurturer, had been forced to leave a job because of her mother's debilitating illness. "I quit to take care of her," she said. Her mother would eventually succumb to the illness, and Dora returned to the welfare office. "I couldn't get back on," she said, "and that's why I'm back out job hunting. They cut me off because I didn't send any paychecks in or something. I didn't know what they were talking about."

Other reasons for partial sanction included failure to cooperate or attend a required program, refusing a job, beginning working, or caseworker error. Moralisia, for example, a Striver who works as a nursing assistant, reported that she had been cut off from welfare for several months in the previous year owing to caseworker error:

> I had consistently dropped off my check stubs at the welfare office, and then I received a letter from Springfield [central office] saying they had cut me off. I called my caseworker's supervisor, crying and explaining my situation. The supervisor told me that it would take 30 days before I was reinstated. After two months and no check, I called my caseworker again. She told me that she had a new boss and that neither she nor the new boss knew anything about the situation, and then hangs up. I didn't know what I was going to do. My childcare copayment had gone up to $33. My rent was past due. I thought to myself, how will I get over this setback? I'm proud of myself, I struggled to meet my family's need and did everything I could to cope. I wrote lists and cut down on the things my kids should have in order to survive.

Another group of fifteen women had received a partial sanction at some point in the year before the interview. Here again, more of those sanctioned were Strivers (47%), followed by Nurturers (33%) and the Disaffected (20%).

The reasons for partial sanction were missed appointments, refusing a job, failing to file paperwork or attend a job program, not cooperating with the rules, or caseworker error. In addition, several respondents did not know the reason for the sanction.

After being sanctioned, nearly equal numbers contested the decision or took no action to reinstate their benefits. Strivers were most likely to fight the sanction, and the Disaffected were least likely to take action against the sanction. These trends may reflect the considerable support of family and friends on which Nurturers and the Disaffected often rely, making contesting the sanction perhaps more work than it's worth. The higher likelihood of a Disaffected not taking action to protest the sanction might also reflect her sense of being overwhelmed by life.

Sanctions did not produce the results that the conservatives had hoped. "Getting tough" with welfare recipients by enforcing the rules for receiving aid did not rid the rolls of cheaters nor push rule violators into the labor market. Sanctions were unassociated with the odds of leaving welfare. Sanctions did increase hardship and were most common among women with multiple problems. Indeed, levels of employment were reduced among the sanctioned. These results suggest that little of benefit to either the sanctioned recipient or society at large was accomplished through the TANF sanctioning process in Illinois. What sanctions did do is identify women with multiple problems who were having a hard time finding employment and following the welfare rules. This unintended result could possibly be of some use to TANF administrators in working with those individuals to overcome the problems that put them in this difficult situation.

CHAPTER 9

Did Welfare Reform Launch the Poor into Better Neighborhoods?

ONE OF THE GLARING DIFFERENCES between Murray, the conservative analyst of welfare reform, and Ellwood, who represents the liberal perspective, in their debate about welfare concerned the place of poor African Americans in the discussion. Murray puts poor urban blacks at the center of his analysis, while Ellwood places them off to the side. The consequences were profound for the debate about PRWORA. In public as well as elite opinion, the plight of ghetto blacks was pivotal. AFDC and associated welfare-state programs (for example, public housing) were seen as trapping African Americans in lives of poverty and degradation. Ellwood, in *Poor Support*, relegates the discussion of poor black communities to one chapter late in the book. He basically argues that the problems of poor blacks constitutes a small percentage (10%) of the poverty problem as he sees it, and is beyond the scope of his analysis. Murray argues in *Losing Ground* that the plight of the urban black community lies at the heart of the problem, and his book revolves around analyzing how welfare state policy affects poor urban African Americans.·

While Ellwood stays away from an analysis of Black urban poverty, there are a group of sociologists, best represented by Douglas Massey and William Julius Wilson, arguing that racism and other "structural" reasons lie at the heart of racial segregation and concentrated poverty in our large cities. This group focuses on the African American experience in cities after the great migration of rural southern African Americans beginning during World War II. Murray, among many other conservative welfare reformers, believes that personal choices and various government disincentives lead to ghetto poverty.

This latter group called for attacking urban poverty by eliminating public housing, long-term welfare payments, and other social supports that they saw as creating perverse incentives to abstain from work and to behave badly. Murray and many of the conservative analysts of welfare reform argued that passing PRWORA and related programs would put poor urban African Americans on the road to success, including moving to better neighborhoods. The argument went something like this: If blacks could break out of the dependency created by AFDC and related programs, they would be motivated to improve their situations. The handcuffs of AFDC and public housing in particular kept poor blacks from moving to better communities.

Liberals predicted the opposite effects from PRWORA. Given the anticipated loss of income that would follow leaving TANF, most recipients would be forced into worse neighborhoods, since they would have less money, liberals said.

In this chapter we track the movements of a sample of urban welfare recipients and see which set of predictions was more on target. In Chicago, and in the IFS sample, poverty is decidedly black. We examined how welfare reform has diluted concentrated poverty and affected residential mobility in Chicago. We examined the residential and income mobility of 403 low-income Chicago families in the years following major reforms in the welfare and public housing systems. Many families received housing vouchers or lived in public housing in addition to receiving welfare. What we found is surprising. Although residents on average moved to slightly lower-poverty neighborhoods as their incomes rose, those neighborhoods were no less racially integrated than their original neighborhoods. In addition, we found considerable ceilings on the degree of improvement, suggesting that Chicago for the near future is likely to remain segregated. The movement off welfare did result in more income for most families, and many did move, but that movement was to only slightly better neighborhoods that were just as segregated as the ones they left. Life got a little better but remained within the confines of urban segregation.

Early Social Disorganization Theory—*Poverty and Neighborhood*

Much urban poverty theory has its origins in early American sociology and particularly in research done at the University of Chicago, which housed the first sociology department in the United States. Many of those first sociologists did their work in Chicago's neighborhoods, focusing largely on the struggles of immigrants as they assimilated to their new home. Whether a study of the Jewish ghetto resident (Wirth, 1928) or the Polish peasant (Thomas & Znaneicki, 1919), the story of how people behaved was told in terms of the social disorganization that groups experienced as they adapted to a new environment. For example, citing migration as a disorganizing force, Robert Park (1936) wrote: "The enormous amount of delinquency, juvenile and adult, that exists today in the Negro communities in northern cities is due in part, though not entirely, to the fact that migrants are not able to accommodate themselves at once to a new and relatively strange environment."

Paralleling the arguments roughly sixty years later, the Chicago School sociologists were attempting to counter the prevailing view that poverty and social problems were the result of intrinsic racial or ethnic personal characteristics that were defective. The Chicago School viewed poverty as a problem that resulted naturally from the growth of cities and the movement of populations in those cities. In this perspective, it was where you lived, not your individual or racial character, that created poverty and other social problems. Transition to a new environment meant that primary relations between family members and extended kin were tested by competing values in the city. The city offered secular, individualistic, and cosmopolitan values that challenged the religious, group, and particularistic norms the immigrants brought with them. These new pressures undermined the authority of—and conformity to—folkways, resulting in deviant behavior. Immigrant communities could not compete with the challenges the big cities presented to young immigrants. Thus, it was the failure of disorganized communities to care and provide for their members that led to poor social conditions (Park & Burgess, 1925). When disorganized communities failed to care for and provide for their members, poor social conditions resulted.

Chicago School theorists argued that the capacity of a disorganized community to care for and meet the needs of its members increased as it assimilated into mainstream society (Park, 1936). As community members adjusted to their new environments and adopted behaviors in line with the mainstream, the barriers between disorganized ethnic enclaves and other communities broke down. Increasing social and economic interaction with mainstream groups meant an increase in the collective resources available for communal needs. It also meant greater mobility for individual community members, bringing new opportunities for jobs and, with increased income, chances to seek housing in neighborhoods with lower levels of poverty. As we show below, this is exactly how reformers in the 1990s in Chicago would again view public housing reform.

Revised Social Disorganization Theory—*Concentrated Poverty*

The advent of the second of the great migrations of African Americans from the South to the North shifted the focus of social disorganization theory from the natural segregation of various ethnic groups to the particular problem of black-white racial segregation in northern cities. In

Chicago following World War II, African Americans flooding to the city from the South were met with acute housing shortages as well as white neighborhoods dedicated to maintaining segregation. Families faced with exorbitant rent for decent housing were forced to accept poor housing conditions or share space to make ends meet. Despite growing public concern about desperate conditions, and a 1948 Supreme Court decision (*Shelley vs. Kraemer,* 1948) striking down restrictive covenants and other explicit forms of racial segregation, Chicago and other major cities remained divided racially. Vast regions of Chicago became populated almost exclusively by African Americans. Many of these neighborhoods developed very high poverty rates and remained racially segregated through the next several decades (Massey & Denton, 1993). This segregation was still evident in our IFS sample, where the highest concentration of poverty was in the largely African American neighborhoods and public housing high-rises.

The persistence of concentrated poverty in African American neighborhoods posed a challenge to social disorganization theorists. Early theorists had described the processes through which communities changed and evolved. However, later scholars were charged with explaining why these families never assimilated and why these poor isolated neighborhoods persisted. William Julius Wilson, working at the University of Chicago at the time, wrote arguably one of the most important books of the time tackling this question. In *The Truly Disadvantaged* (1987), he argued as follows:

> The residents of highly concentrated poverty neighborhoods in the inner city today not only infrequently interact with those individuals or families who have had a stable work history and have had little involvement with welfare or public assistance, they also seldom have sustained contact with friends or relatives in the more stable areas of the city or in the suburbs. The net result is that the degree of social isolation—defined in this context as the lack of contact or of sustained interaction with individuals and institutions that represent mainstream society—in these highly concentrated poverty areas has become far greater than we had previously assumed.

In Wilson's view the residents of concentrated poverty neighborhoods, "the urban underclass," were socially and economically isolated. They lacked access to vital economic networks that carry information about jobs and to gainfully employed role models. In the absence of real prospects for economic advancement, youth embraced antisocial behaviors; they dropped out of school, had children without marrying, shunned the formal labor market, and turned to crime. Wilson's work focused attention on "concentrated poverty" neighborhoods—in this case, African American neighborhoods—which have subsequently come to be defined by others as neighborhoods with poverty rates of 40 percent or higher. Wilson proposed a broad package of universal benefits to help eliminate the problems of concentrated poverty.

By his logic, lifting people out of poverty would naturally result in a reduction in both economic and racial segregation (Wilson, 1987).

Douglas Massey and his colleagues shared Wilson's focus on concentrated poverty but disagreed with his assessment that racial desegregation would naturally follow poverty reduction. Massey & Denton's analysis (1993) characterized Chicago as one of the nation's "hypersegregated" urban areas, and Massey & Fischer (2000) argued that racial segregation was the key factor behind the rise in concentrated poverty. Any successful effort to end the problems of concentrated poverty, they argued, must explicitly address the dual problems of racial and economic segregation. In their view, concentrated poverty could not be eliminated without policies designed to disrupt racial discrimination in private housing markets and institutionalized processes of neighborhood racial succession (Massey & Denton, 1993). Given the results of our study presented below, this view seems especially prescient.

Although they disagreed on the best approach to addressing the problem of concentrated poverty in African American neighborhoods, Wilson and Massey would both agree that outside forces, not individual behavior, shaped community. Segregation itself produced problem behaviors. In both formulations the goal was to shift the focus from explanations that highlighted deviant behaviors to an emphasis on the external forces that caused them. Moreover, in both views, racial segregation, economic segregation, and poverty were inextricably linked.

The Conservative Perspective—*Backlash against Government Intervention*

Though social disorganization theories played a key role in defining and framing the focus on urban poverty in the 1980s and 1990s, they were not the only influential school of thought. A conservative perspective saw government policies, rather than the interaction between outside forces of racial and economic segregation, as the cause of persistent urban poverty. As we outlined in the first chapter, conservative critics reacted to the breadth of the New Deal and Great Society programs such as AFDC and called for attacking urban poverty by eliminating public housing, long-term welfare payments, and other social supports that they saw as creating perverse incentives to abstain from work and to behave badly. They argued that welfare policy, and public housing policy in particular, had concentrated the poor, trapping them in governmentally created ghettos and distorting their motivations to conform to mainstream norms.

Although liberal and conservative theorists argued about what was cause and what was effect, they agreed that the situation in concentrated poverty neighborhoods had become intolerable. The result of this convergence was a package of reforms that sought to drastically reduce dependence on public support. While liberals were not keen on cutting off this aid, they were caught on the horns of a dilemma they had helped to create by agreeing that it would take drastic action to ameliorate the problem of concentrated poverty in these communities. The Quality Housing and Work Responsibility Act (QHWRA), passed in 1998, introduced major reforms to the public housing system. Like PRWORA, it devolved power to the local level while imposing a requirement that recipients of state aid work outside the home. In the name of ending housing dependency, eliminating unsafe housing, and reducing concentrated poverty, the act gave housing authorities leeway to replace some existing public housing developments with a combination of mixed-income housing developments and vouchers that would provide government subsidies for private-market housing. Whereas PRWORA sought to disrupt the cyclical disadvantage associated with concentrated poverty, provisions of QHWRA offered a means of dispersing low-income families across a wider range of neighborhoods, thereby directly attacking concentrated poverty itself.

Chicago and the state wholeheartedly embraced the welfare and public housing reforms. Following the passage of QHWRA, Chicago implemented a plan, which is still under way today, to demolish high-rise public-housing developments and disperse their residents (CHA, 2000). Displaced families were given housing choice vouchers, and mixed-income communities were rapidly built on the sites of the old housing developments. Thus, the economic and residential trajectories of low-income Chicago families were partially shaped by reforms that sought to disrupt both dependence on state aid and concentrated poverty. Indeed, from the conservative perspective, Chicago presents a best-case scenario for the deconcentration hypothesis. Given the large reductions in TANF participation and the almost complete demolition of the Chicago Public Housing Authority projects, poor African Americans had a very good chance of breaking the hold of those supposedly demoralizing federal programs and moving into the American mainstream.

To determine whether policies such as QHWRA and TANF were having the desired effect, we examined the economic and residential trajectories of low-income Chicago families in the post-welfare world, following them as they dispersed to other, sometimes better, neighborhoods as their incomes rose. We also determined whether their moves led them to more integrated neighborhoods—in effect determining whether welfare policy is having an effect on concentrated poverty in Chicago.

Study Description

The IFS sample used in this study consisted of the 403 Chicago respondents who were available during each of the three interviews (1999–2000, 2000–

2001, and 2001–2002) and who lived within the boundaries of the city of Chicago. As with the larger IFS sample, the sample is largely single mothers who have low levels of education and multiple children and who received public assistance for multiple years.[1] More than 30 percent of the sample received some form of government housing assistance, with 15 percent living in public housing and 16 percent holding housing vouchers. In examining residential mobility, we relied on only the 183 sample members who changed census tracts during the study period.

To track neighborhood changes, we asked IFS members a set of questions, ranging from years living in their current residence, to attitudes toward safety in and satisfaction with their neighborhood, to (self-reported) household income.[2] We also geo-coded the new and old addresses to identify the census tract where each respondent lived. This allowed us to connect census data on percentage of neighborhood residents living below the poverty level, median household income, percentage non-Hispanic black, and percentage non-Hispanic white.

We gauged the effect of welfare policy on income by measuring (self-reported) income at the outset of the study and following families for three years, holding constant several background and family characteristics known to also affect income.[3] The key question we asked was, Who is affected most by the policies? If those with the highest initial incomes see the most income growth, then policies are beneficial to the most capable or stable families. On the other hand, if those with the highest incomes see the least growth in income, then the policies likely have a ceiling effect. We also similarly assessed the effects of welfare policy on neighborhood conditions, determining whether IFS members moved to neighborhoods with higher or lower concentrations of African American or white residents and higher or lower levels of poverty. We also determined whether the choice of neighborhood differs by initial neighborhood characteristics and again looked for a ceiling effect limiting the levels of integration achieved in the new neighborhoods. Finally, we assessed whether the background characteristics of movers differed systematically from those of nonmovers. The characteristics reviewed include age, age at the birth of a first child, number and age of children, education of mother, years on welfare, employed or not, years living in current address, whether living in public housing or having a housing voucher, median household income in the neighborhood, neighborhood poverty level, racial distribution (percentage white or black), and attitude toward neighborhood (fear, satisfaction).

Finally, to gain additional insight into the characteristics of movers, we used a second sample of five hundred IFS respondents, half of whom were living in public housing and half of whom were not (but were still poor and receiving welfare). We tracked changes in residence over two years and looked for differences between public housing residents and the other low-income families.

Context of Poverty in Chicago

The poverty rate in Chicago fell by 2 percent between 1990 and 2000; this general decline in poverty rate was also accompanied by a decline in concentrated poverty in Chicago neighborhoods.[4] On average, community areas with low 1990 poverty rates experienced slight increases in poverty, while those with high 1990 poverty levels saw reductions. In 1990 some communities had poverty rates greater than 60 percent, with the poorest community reporting a poverty rate of 75 percent. In contrast, by 2000 no community area had a poverty rate above 55 percent.[5] All community areas with 1990 poverty rates greater than 45 percent had lower poverty rates by 2000. Thus, concentrated poverty was breaking up in the years leading to the IFS study. However, racial segregation persisted. Although some communities experienced large shifts in their racial makeup, they were the anomalies.[6] Of seventy-seven community areas in Chicago, fifty-four have a population that is either more than 90 percent or less than 10 percent black.

As described in Chapter 5, IFS sample members saw sizable income growth over the study period, although there appears to be a distinct ceiling effect in play. The higher the income at the first interview, the less the person's income grew over the study period. While those with higher incomes topped out and began to see income loss at some point, those with the lowest incomes experienced the most growth.

Residential Mobility of the IFS Sample

The sample members at the initial interview were concentrated in communities to the south and west of the city center that were primarily African American and had high levels of poverty (see table 9.1). One-fourth of the sample lived in neighborhoods with greater than 98 percent black residents, and more than one-half lived in neighborhoods with a black population of 95 percent or greater. The pattern is less striking but still visible for economic segregation. More than three-quarters of the IFS sample lived in neighborhoods with higher poverty rates and lower median household income than the average Chicago neighborhood, and more than three-fourths lived in census tracts with a median household income lower than that of the average Chicago resident.

We also found that sample members not only live in community areas with the highest rates of poverty and black residents but also live in the census tracts within those neighborhoods that have the highest poverty rates and the highest proportion of black residents (table 9.1, column 2). Because analyses using community areas as the neighborhood unit would understate segregation and the concentration of poverty, we use census tracts as the neighborhood unit in the subsequent analyses.

TABLE 9.1—Wave 1 Neighborhood Characteristics

	COMMUNITY AREA	CENSUS TRACT
	Mean (standard deviation)	*Mean (standard deviation)*
% Black	68 (35)	75 (36)
% White	12 (17)	6 (13)
% Poverty	34 (19)	36 (21)
Median income	$30,489 (9,600)	$27,355 (11,769)

Study participants were quite mobile over the course of the study, with 46 percent of sample members moving at least once during the study period. Differences between movers and nonmovers were statistically significant in only four instances. The odds of moving were higher among those with less education and higher household income, and the odds were lower for those with housing vouchers and longer tenure in their original neighborhoods, as shown in table 9.2. (Column 2 in table 9.2 shows the factors that increased or decreased the odds of moving. Values greater than 1 represent higher odds of moving, and values less than 1 represent lower odds. Therefore, those with less than a high school education were 57 percent more likely to move than those who had graduated from high school. Those who had lived in their original neighborhoods for a longer period were 90 percent less likely to move than those with shorter tenures.)

On average, IFS sample members were able to move to neighborhoods whose poverty rates were approximately 8 percent lower and median household incomes were $2,832 higher than in their initial neighborhoods (table 9.3). However, a ceiling effect is apparent, with the tipping points at 28 percent for neighborhood poverty rates and $29,317 for median neighborhood income. Those who resided initially in neighborhoods with poverty rates less than 28 percent moved to *higher*-poverty neighborhoods, and those living initially in neighborhoods with poverty rates higher than 28 percent moved to lower-poverty neighborhoods. Moreover, the analyses suggest a potential for reconcentration of poverty in those neighborhoods where median household income was approximately $29,000 in 2000 and where the neighborhood poverty rate was nearly 30 percent.

Study participants did not move to neighborhoods with significantly higher white populations or lower African American populations (table 9.2). Racial segregation was reinforced by the moves. There is only a 1 percentage

TABLE 9.2—Odds of Moving by Individual Characteristics

	Odds ratios (Exp(B))
Age at first birth	.99 (.03)
Number of children	.95 (.08)
% With some college	.78 (.31)
% Less than high school	1.57 (.27)[+]
Household income (effect of thousand dollar change)	1.04 (.02)*
% With: all children under age 11	1.50 (.28)
All children under age 5	1.35 (.34)
% Nonblack	.68 (.49)
Years on welfare	1.05 (.07)
% Working for pay	.89 (.23)
Years in residence	.90 (.03)***
% In public housing	.81 (.39)
% With housing voucher	.46 (.34)*
Attitude toward neighborhood	1.05 (.14)
% Black (effect of 10 percent change)	.93 (.06)
% White	[a]
% In poverty (effect of 10 percent change)	1.29 (.09) **
Median household income	[a]

[+] $p <= 0.10$, *$p <= 0.05$, **$p <= 0.01$, ***$p <= 0.001$, [a] omitted for sake of parsimony

point increase in the average percentage of whites in the new neighborhood and a 2 point decline in percentage of blacks. The ceiling effect (at 71%) also indicates that future residential moves will likely not remedy this segregation. Of all the movers in our sample, 64 percent achieved very little change in neighborhood racial characteristics by moving; they relocated to neighborhoods where the percentage of black residents is within 5 percent of its value in their initial neighborhood. The remaining 36 percent were split further into two categories, with one-half moving from predominantly African American neighborhoods (more than 95% black) to neighborhoods of varying racial makeup, and the other half moving from neighborhoods of varying racial makeup to neighborhoods with predominantly African

TABLE 9.3—Relationship between Residential Mobility and Initial Neighborhood Characteristics (for Movers Only)

	NEIGHBORHOOD CHARACTERISTICS			
	% in Poverty	Median Household Income	% Black	% White
Third interview level	.29 (.01)***	29,103 (837)***	.73 (.03)***	.08 (.01)***
Annual change (slope, at mean wave 1 level)	.04 (.01)***	1,416 (572)*	-.01 (.02)	.01 (.01)
Effect of interview 1 level on slope	-.44 (.02)***	-.45 (.02)***	-.46 (.02)***	-.44 (.02)***
Wave 1 mean level	.36	26,166	.74	.07
Zero Slope Point	.28	29,317	.71	.08

$^+p < 0.10$, $^*p < 0.05$, $^{**}p < 0.01$, $^{***}p < 0.001$

Americans. Thus, although some individual sample members did realize significant changes in neighborhood racial characteristics by moving, the movement of some people to racially mixed neighborhoods is balanced by the movement of others to African American neighborhoods. The net effect is one of no change in racial segregation.

Behind the Scenes in Families' Decisions to Relocate

One would think that, given the opportunity, those living in low-income neighborhoods, with their typically higher crime rates and dysfunction, would want to relocate. And indeed many do seek other neighborhoods. Income obviously makes a difference in mobility. Those with higher incomes were more likely to relocate, but the neighborhoods they moved to, on average, were rarely fundamentally different from the ones they left. Our qualitative interviews with IFS respondents shed some light on this conundrum. In many instances, it seems, residents may have become inured to the crime in their neighborhoods. Perhaps this, coupled with the social isolation they experience by rarely venturing far from their neighborhoods, makes them see few alternatives to their current situation.

When we think about "bad" neighborhoods, it is crime that most frequently springs to mind. Interestingly, however, those living in high-crime neighborhoods are often the least worried about crime (Furstenberg, 1971). Although people may perceive a situation as risky, they are not necessarily afraid (Ferraro, 1995). Perhaps, as some research suggests, those unused to crime fear it the most, because fear is really the fear of the strange and unknown. If what we fear is the strange and unknown, a new unknown neighborhood may appear scarier than a known high-crime neighborhood. °In our interviews with approximately seventy IFS respondents, we found that only 13 percent were afraid in their current neighborhoods, even though 70 percent of the sample resided in neighborhoods with pervasive crime. About one-third lived in particularly violent areas. Furthermore, only 8 percent were angry about the conditions. Most people in this group suggest that crime and dangers are rather ordinary and no more likely than other threats in life. As Vicky, age 29 and a resident of a violent neighborhood, said, "I'm used to stuff like this. I've been here 11 years. My old neighborhood was like this, too." Or as another resident said, "I don't think I need to move. All neighborhoods are dangerous in one way or another. I used to think I should move to the suburbs, but really, they have the same things going on there . . . it's just more secret."

Using another slice of the IFS data involving approximately five hundred low-income families, we compared the odds of moving between those in public housing in Chicago (typically high-rise, concentrated public housing) and those in market-rate housing. Both groups received welfare. We found that public housing families were less likely to move than non-public-housing families. Only about one in five public housing families moved out of public housing between 1999 and 2001. In contrast, about one-third of those not in public housing moved. In fact, the relative odds of moving among respondents who lived in public housing in 1999 were 70 percent less than for their counterparts living outside of public housing, controlling for a variety of other personal and neighborhood variables, including employment, total household income, number of children, perception of neighborhood as safe and good/bad place to raise children, and neighbors willing to help, among others.

Of course, this is not to suggest that no one in high-crime neighborhoods preferred to move. Many in fact did move, although, as we note above, the moves were not to significantly improved situations. Coupled with the qualitative data we have discussed, these findings suggest that perhaps the years of segregation (by race and income) have taken a psychic and economic toll on many families.

Discussion

The findings suggest that the trend toward economic integration among the IFS sample is nearing a point of equilibrium and, by extension, they suggest that the additional deconcentration of poverty, if any, is likely to be small among this group. Continuing to rely on deconcentration strategies will have limited success. Moreover, racial segregation seems unaffected by these trends. The average sample member who moved saw no change in neighborhood racial makeup, and our analyses suggest little reason to expect poverty deconcentration to achieve racial integration. The pattern seen in the IFS sample mirrors that seen in Chicago as a whole between 1990 and 2000: There was a reduction in concentrated poverty, but there was not a similar reduction in racial segregation. Based on these results, a cynical reader might argue that policy changes implemented in the last half of the 1990s yielded only small improvements in economic status for the poor and did so without upsetting the racial subordination that has figured so prominently in the history of poverty in urban areas. While the reforms of the 1990s improved the quality of life for poor Chicagoans, they failed to attack the institutionalized processes and structures that perpetuate racial and economic segregation. Perhaps Massey and Wilson, with their perspective on enduring structural reasons for poverty and social isolation, were right. Additionally, the problems of the very poor welfare recipient are visited on poor African American communities. The more well-off white neighborhoods avoid having to meet the challenges that these poor families face. The twin policies of welfare reform and public housing deconcentration improve the lives of the very poor but do so without substantially modifying the economic and racial order of the city, at least in Chicago.

CHAPTER 10

Assessing the Results and
Moving Forward

TEN YEARS AGO there were two competing lenses through which to observe welfare reform. Figure 10.1 limns the two approaches. Following the work of Murray and Ellwood, we have sketched out how each side would "see" welfare reform working out. For the conservatives, welfare reform meant an improvement in the lives of the poor who had been trapped by AFDC. AFDC and other related programs had kept recipients, especially the urban African American poor, trapped in a set of incentives that made them dependent and isolated. The reform meant a better life. Once off welfare, and here the sanctions used to get them off served the recipient well, the person would find work. Work would lead to more income that in turn would lead to a better neighborhood and in all likelihood a better school for the person's sons or daughters. Leaving welfare would raise the person's spirits as they joined the mainstream, more income would reduce stress, and one's mental health would improve. These improvements would come while spending on welfare would be held in check, producing better lives with no new spending (see figure 10.1, bottom).

For the liberal, the picture looked very different. Since poverty was the result of low wages, little job availability, and disability, the removal from welfare would have negative results for the person. AFDC was not the cause of poverty. Removing the person from aid would only reduce the income available and make things worse for the family. Since PRWORA did nothing to increase the wage paid to the poor person (indeed it might suppress wages), did nothing to increase the number of jobs available, and did nothing to remedy any disability the person suffered from, removal from support would only put the person at a distinct disadvantage. Sanctions would push TANF recipients with the most problems off the rolls, making

FIGURE 10.1—Summary of Competing Paradigms

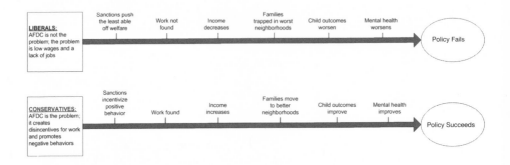

their lives worse. Income would fall for most people. They would be less able to stay in their home as income dropped, and the stress of less income would lead to worse mental health. The sons and daughters of the poor person would suffer in school because of these factors (see figure 10.1, top). Conservatives predicted success for the poor while liberals saw only negatives from the reform. One well-known liberal reformer called PRWORA "the worst thing Bill Clinton has done" (Edelman, 1997). The analysis in this book cannot ultimately settle the issue. We don't know, and cannot know, how our sample would have done if the counterfactual prevailed. Where would our sample have been if welfare reform had not been signed into law? How would the women in the sample have done if the *status quo ante* had prevailed? We simply cannot know and therefore cannot say with certainty that the policies in question had the influence we say they did. We have tried to persuade the reader of the importance of how policy shaped the person, but as we have also argued, the influence runs the other way too; different types of persons react to policies in different ways. We hope we have been persuasive, but the analysis is limited by what might have been.

The preceding nine chapters analyzed the impact of that reform on a random sample of people who were on welfare when the reform was put into practice in Illinois. We have tracked those people over time, adding in-depth qualitative interviews to our quantitative analysis. We can see from the evidence presented here how the two approaches compare in predicting the impact of the reform. Our work was made possible by the foresight of a young state senator who wanted to move beyond the tired rhetoric of left and right in assessing how the reform affected people in Illinois. We have kept Obama's perspective in mind as we have done our analysis. If we made sensible assumptions about whom we were studying and how long and how well those people needed to be tracked, we could better understand both the impact of the reform and the factors that contributed to the poverty in question. We could remove the blinders of the ideological debates of the '80s and '90s. We could look at the problems of the poor with a clearer sense of what problems people have and what we can do about them. That is what we have tried to do in this book. In this final chapter we will review our results and evaluate the two competing paradigms. Our goal is to point the way to a fresher approach to tackling the problems of poverty in our society.

We begin by suggesting that neither perspective had the story completely correct. Figure 10.2 highlights our results as they relate to the liberal and conservative paradigms. PRWORA changed the lives of the people who had been on welfare when the reform began. TANF was not a safety net in the ways that AFDC was. Each state determined for itself how much temporary support a young poor mother could get and under what conditions that support would be offered. In Illinois, the TANF rolls have been reduced substantially, from over 200,000 cases when the reform was implemented to somewhere around 10% of that figure today.

Welfare is no longer a way of life in Illinois and a great many other states. But the situation that has been produced is a far cry from the vision conservatives had a decade ago. Our person-centered approach shines a light on a situation that leaves many of the most vulnerable adrift in a world of scarcity and risk. While income did grow for the average person we studied, and many of the catastrophic consequences predicted by liberals clearly did not emerge (increases in child poverty and homelessness, for example), the world of the poor mother remained one in which work was often hard to find. Half of our sample was not in the labor market four years after we began tracking them. Work did not replace welfare. Work did not seem to be related to time on welfare, as many conservatives had thought.

The notion that recipients sank into some kind of deep dependency due to time on welfare was not borne out by our analysis of the predictors of work. Human capital was the key to work, although our sample was trapped at the very low end of the labor market even when they were working. Sanctions too seemed to belie the conservative approach. Sanctioning the people that broke rules did not lead to their exiting welfare and was associated with hardships. The removal of AFDC made individual level factors more important in the lives of the poor. AFDC was a real problem, but removing it did not make the problems disappear. Mental health issues are a case on point.

Finally, educational outcomes for the children in our sample proved complicated and important. Work for mothers seemed to have a negative affect on boys but not girls. On the bright side, girls seemed to be unaffected by the mother's work. However, the impact on boys is clearly troubling and suggests the need for more support for the children of working mothers. The picture that emerges shows that AFDC was more of a problem than liberals admitted, but that removing it made the advantages of human capital more important. Building that capital in people would take more support along the lines adumbrated in the Illinois approach (EITC, Medicaid, and other supports for the low wage earner). Many of the most vulnerable were left behind.

PRWORA was a watershed in American social policy. The policy and its relative success opens the door to more innovation. Ironically, the success of this conservative reform makes a conservative analysis less useful as we move forward. Once the federal program (AFDC) has been removed, our gaze must shift to the lives of the poor and the factors (both person-centered and otherwise) that limit opportunity. This means developing research strategies that trace the differences between individuals as they are affected by a broad range of factors.

Our person-centered research brings us closer to the populations we are studying. We have tried to remove the ideological blinders of the past generation in our analysis. We can see more clearly the individuals we hope to understand. Methodologies should be chosen as a way of closing the distance between the researcher and the groups we are studying. This is especially true as these marginalized groups are included in society by new social policies. Welfare reform did not end the plight of the poor, nor did it assign these poor to a life of destitution. What it did do was make the personal resources and problems of the individual more important. People

FIGURE 10.2—Summary of Results in the Context of Competing Paradigms

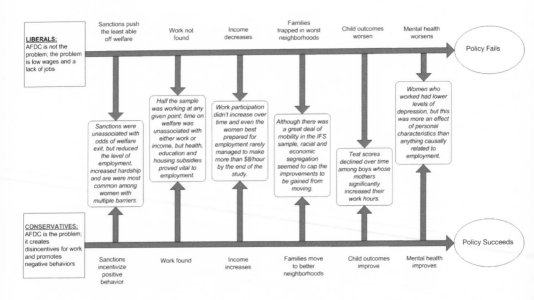

with few personal resources were at a distinct disadvantage, and that was reflected in how they managed once AFDC was eliminated.

Although ideological debates will always have a place in policy research, we have come to a point when it is simply not enough to grasp the change process of those individuals whose lives we want to change. Our reliance over the last three decades on program evaluations and environmental assumptions about human nature have led to a kind of research that overestimates the importance of formal program goals and the ability of implementers to achieve them. This style of research underestimates the differences between people and how factors outside the intervention shape how much we do and do not change. If our policy-making is to be based on holding people accountable for what they do, then it might behoove policy makers to understand how the people we want to change think about what they do. Policy analysis should, therefore, move toward research designs that put the person back at the center of inquiry and make him or her less of a stranger to policy makers. PRWORA was about removing a bad policy (AFDC) and making people stand on their own two feet. The research strategies that attend these reforms must give us a clear vision of what makes some stand tall and others falter.

People can be stubborn, selfless, self-defeating, innovative, adaptable, and contradictory. Their outlook and disposition are shaped by their experiences, their interpretations, and their identities. Maybe the differences in program outcomes arise because *individuals* are reacting differently to interventions. Maybe people behave in a way that is consistent with their "story" of who they are, rather than simply as rational calculators. The understanding of welfare reform lay far outside the parameters set by the liberals and conservatives of an earlier generation, for this new world requires new thinking.

Blank (2007), working from a conventional liberal perspective, honestly reflects the situation.

> Thus, I find myself struck by the following conundrum: On the one hand, the movement off public assistance and into work was far greater than I would have guessed possible in such a short period of time. Even with multiple synergies between welfare reform, EITC expansion, economic expansion and other changes, I would not have guessed such rapid behavioral change would have occurred among single mothers. On the other hand, given that such dramatic changes did occur, I am surprised at how little they have affected other domains of life for these women. I would have guessed that such dramatic labor market changes would have fed through to greater changes in other behaviors. Certainly, there is continuing grist for the research mill of social scientists in all disciplines to understand both why one set of behaviors was so responsive in the past decade, while other behaviors have been relatively unchanged.

Our framework and results lead us to a different conclusion. Figure 10.2 illustrates the main findings of this book and places them in the context of the liberal and conservative paradigms. Can it be that policy and the person both matter? That is what we seem to be finding. Plato made a similar point more than two thousand years ago.

> We must admit that the same elements and characters that appear in the state must exist in every one of us; where else could they have come from? It would be absurd to imagine that among peoples with a reputation for a high-spirited character, like the Thracians and Scythians and northerners generally, the states have not derived that character from their individual members; or that it is otherwise with the love of knowledge, which would be ascribed chiefly to our own part of the world, or with the love of money, which one would specially connect with Phoenicia and Egypt. (XIII: IV.435)

Plato was suggesting that the structure of the polis, what we would now call policy, produced the character of the citizen, that is the person, and that different types of persons shaped policy. Plato ties the person to the polity in a dialectical fashion with the influence moving in both directions. This perspective connects the structure of the self to the structure of the government. The isomorphism (a sameness of structure) between policy and person goes a long way to explaining what we found in Illinois. Plato asserts that in the same way that a state will be just only if it is ordered properly, so too will an individual be just only if he or she is guided by virtues that exist in the proper amount and order. In this view, the policy and person are dialectically merged such that a democratic polity nurtures a certain kind of person, whose psyche, in turn, reinforces the government. There is no doubt that our contemporary social science methods would be inadequate to testing the Platonic notion empirically. Still it seems that much of what we find about welfare reform suggests that state policies are linked to personal outcomes in a very complex way: the political culture of the state produces policies that, if they comport to the personal attributes of the citizen, seem to have powerful, if difficult to measure, impacts. Likewise, if the state has a fair number of providers constituting its poor, then those policies will support the desire for work and inclusion in the mainstream.

Human capital matters, but so does the context in which that capital manifests itself (policy). While the policy does shape the person (moving her off welfare and for many into the labor market), the person also shapes the policy (half of the sample, while off welfare, does not participate in the labor market). The person's sense of self and her strengths will determine how she does in this market-driven environment, and those with fewer personal resources will continue to fare poorly while those with more resources will fare better. The latter group will be limited by the structures of race, class, and gender, which still shape life chances in America. We can see that even under the best circumstances, in which incomes moved up and people moved to slightly better communities, the policy did not transform the distribution of life chances. These kinds of changes may be the best we can hope for. But there is half the sample that has fallen into a policy shadow world. No longer dependent on the old AFDC program but not quite a part of the mainstream, it is this group that is caught in the new shadow land of policy analysis. Less poor than before and using fewer public benefits, this group is dependent on family and friends to care for children and self. Welfare reform has shifted the responsibility to the private sector, where many think it should be. But surely an underclass hiding in the shadows is not the result we want. It is this territory between public and private, in what we might call the civic or community terrain, where the hard work of inclusion will take place in the decade to come.

There is an extremely important upside to this situation. With few on welfare anymore, it is hard to blame welfare for the problems of the poor. Women who are raising children on their own now share a set of problems that bring them together despite differences of race, region, and, to some extent, income. There is no welfare group to stigmatize. Additionally, welfare reform—at least by our measures—is a success. Income increased for the group who had to transition off relief. Very few people were worse off four years later. The average person was significantly better off. These are real benefits to the reform and they were accomplished with no increases in spending. Getting people off AFDC turned out to be a very good thing to do in Illinois. But the problems people had did not disappear with AFDC. Indeed, without welfare to fight about, we might actually be able to see the people that need help and "wrap around" those individuals the resources they need to live productive lives as citizens. With the person and her needs in front of us, we can see what combination of supports and resources is needed to move her and her children into the mainstream of American society. We can do this if we put the old ideological battles of right and left behind us and look through a new prism at problems and strengths of the poor. Welfare reform has brought us a new day, but one that neither the liberals nor the conservatives could have imagined when the world of social policy was shaped by their battles a decade ago. Ideologies created frameworks that distorted how we saw the lives of the poor. Person-centered research can help us see beyond the tired ideas of the past.

Springfield Data Collection

Interviews with politicians and policy advocates were administered over a four-year period (1999–2003) by a team of students working under my supervision. The objective of the data collection was to describe the opinion leaders' welfare reform activities from the initial design period through the implementation of the Illinois TANF program. Two undergraduate honors theses (by Janice Law and Elissa Koch) and one dissertation (by Christine George) were the result of these efforts. Each student was charged with using open-ended interview techniques to capture the activities of key leaders. A sample of key informants was developed based on expert opinion and legislative committee chairmanships. The informants were interviewed three times over the four-year period. While there was some variation in the overall data collection depending on the student's focus, all interviews covered the issues described in the appended protocols. Interviewers were trained to pursue issues that evolved in the course of the interview. Field notes were taken on all interviews and were coded for salient categories.

Background on the IFS Qualitative Sample

Qualitative methods have proven very useful in understanding the lives of the poor. Especially during the period from 1950 to 1980, we learned that behaviors that often looked irrational or pathological made a great deal of sense once the observer put herself in the position of the poor person. We hope to draw upon tradition to illuminate what the lives of the poor are like under welfare reform and to help state leaders think through the best ways to accomplish the goals of that reform, especially by creating meaningful independence from welfare and success in the labor market.

We have begun this process with what we call "person-centered policy analysis." We look at variations amongst individuals in how they are affected by policies, and we look carefully at what the person brings to the situation (Lewis & Maruna, 1998). In this approach, the concept of identity is very important. One's identity will determine, to a large degree, how an individual makes sense out of a policy and adapts to it. Here we return to Rainwater's classic formulation of identity as "who the individual believes himself to be and to be becoming." It is that conception of self, we will argue, that shapes how the person understands welfare reform and what that person does in response to it. While Rainwater was interested in explaining how that identity is formed amongst the African American poor, we were more interested in demonstrating how that formed identity then shapes consequent action. It is this identity of the welfare recipient that shapes how one reacts to the constraints of welfare reform.

Sample

The sample for this qualitative study was randomly drawn from a sample of 750 welfare recipients living in the city of Chicago. The initial selection included 150 individuals who were contacted by letter, and then by telephone or in person, to participate in the study. Sixty-nine agreed to be interviewed in the summer of 2000 (corresponding to a response rate of 46 percent of the initial drawing) and this number was reduced to 58 in 2001 (corresponding to a response rate of 39 percent). The current study uses these 58 respondents, for whom information is accessible for both waves of interviews.

Despite the low response rates, t tests comparing the citywide sample with the qualitative one revealed no significant differences in several domains considered: age, education, ethnicity, employment, work experience, and welfare status. The only significant difference between the two samples resulted from the fact that the citywide sample included more men than the qualitative study. Aside from this difference, the sample for the qualitative study was representative of the welfare population living in Chicago. table B.1 shows the sample composition of this study.

In a total of 58 interviews, all but one of the respondents were female (98 percent) and the great majority were African Americans (about 85 percent of the sample), even though other ethnicities appeared in the sample as well: whites (10 percent), Hispanics or Latinos (3 percent), and one Native American (2 percent). The age range of this sample, starting with 18 years old, was rather broad, with most individuals being 20 to 30 years old (41 percent) or 31 to 40 years old (35 percent). In terms of education, 50 percent of the respondents had 12 or more years of school, while the other 50 percent had less than 12 years. The number of children per family also varied between 1 and 7; most respondents had either 1 child (30 percent) or 2 children (36 percent). Table B.1 indicates that the majority of individuals in our sample were currently employed (67 percent).

Analysis

Each transcript of the 58 interviews was coded twice, independently, and then the content was analyzed by two different researchers. The analysis started with four categories, according to the respondents' status with respect to welfare and work: on welfare/on work; on welfare/off work; off welfare/on work; and off welfare/off work. Through content analysis, themes began emerging, and a new categorization, based on the following domains, was necessary: children, sources of social support, social relationships, and life difficulties. The fact that two waves of information on the same person are available in two different periods of time (summer of 2000 and summer of 2001) rendered this analysis particularly rich by making accessible not only attitudes and intentions but actual behaviors. This additional information made a kind of a kind of triangulation possible, which added to the reliability of the results.

TABLE B.1—Sample Composition

		Frequencies	*Percentages*
Gender	Male	1	2%
	Female	57	98%
Ethnicity	Black	49	85%
	White	6	10%
	Hispanic	2	3%
	Native American	1	2%
Years of Age	Sample Average	34	
	Under 19	3	5%
	20 to 30	24	41%
	31 to 40	20	35%
	41 to 50	9	16%
	51 and older	2	3%
Years of Education	Sample Average	12	
	Less than 12	29	50%
	12	7	12%
	13 to 14	13	23%
	15 to 16	6	10%
	17 and more	3	5%
Number of Children	Sample Average	2.5	
	One	17	30%
	Two	21	36%
	Three	6	10%
	Four or more	14	24%
Number Employed		39	67%
Public Aid Benefits	Welfare	10	17%
	Food stamps and/ or Medicaid	37	64%
Total		58	100%

We divided our sample into three main categories of welfare recipients based on how individuals discussed work and family: (1) Nurturers, (2) Providers, and (3) Disaffected. Providers structure their lives, to a greater or lesser degree, around employment. We identified two main types of Providers: a) Strivers, who are the steady ladder climbers and the intermittent

TABLE B.2—Comparison of Types of Welfare Recipients on Selected Variables

	Nurturers n=11 (19%)	Providers n=41 (71%)		Disaffected n=6 (10%)
		Strivers n=27 (46%)	Reluctant n=14 (24%)	
Years of Age (Group average)	34	31	31	39
Years of Education (Group average)	13	12	11	12
Number of children (Group average)	2	2	3	2
Working	0%	89%	100%	29%
In School for Career	0%	11%	0%	0%
On Welfare (TANF)	27%	11%	8%	42%
Food Stamps Only	9%	26%	8%	0%
Medicaid Only	18%	7%	8%	0%
Food Stamps and/or Medicaid	55%	26%	46%	57%
No Benefits (Food Stamps, Medicaid)	18%	41%	38%	43%

career seekers, and b) Reluctant Providers, who work only out of necessity. Nurturers place their children and family relationships first. The Disaffected appear generally overwhelmed by both family issues and work demands. We reviewed all responses from those interviewed and placed everyone in one of the three main categories. Table B.2 depicts the three identities we found based on a number of policy variables.

Providers constituted by far the largest group of individuals (71 percent), while the Disaffected represented only 10 percent of the sample. Providers all worked or were involved in school full-time in the pursuit of education for career purposes. In sharp contrast with this group, Nurturers did not participate in the official workforce, and only 29 percent of the Disaffected were employed. Members of all groups were still receiving cash benefits, although there were fewer recipients among the Providers than among the other two groups. All groups also received food stamps and Medicaid, alone or in combination, but the group with the most members receiving these benefits was the Nurturers.

The average age was the same (31 years old) among both types of Providers (Strivers and Reluctant). The Nurturers were older (an average age of 34 years), and the Disaffected were considerably older (an average age of 39 years). The level of education did not differ much from group to group, Nurturers being on average the most well educated (an average of 13 years of school) and Reluctant Providers being the least schooled (an average of 11 years). The average number of children was about the same for all groups, although a little bigger for Reluctant Providers, who averaged 3.

Most of our sample has left welfare. Nurturers and Providers achieve independence in different ways. Most respondents transitioned to the world of work (71 percent of the sample are Providers).

A third of Providers (the Reluctant ones) participated in the labor force only reluctantly, suggesting that this is the group affected by the 1996 reform. Between Reluctant Providers and Nurturers, 43 percent of our population relied on means other than committed participation in the labor force to advance self-sufficiency. This result is not driven by a lack of goals or initiative. Reluctant Providers prefer to be like Nurturers and channel their efforts into homemaking and child rearing. Given external sources of support, Reluctant Providers would most likely elect to become Nurturers. In the same fashion, Nurturers would probably become Reluctant Providers if financial support was withdrawn. In both cases identity drives behavior, with policy having a limited but important affect on incentives.

Policy reforms have made the greatest impact on Reluctant Providers, who, lacking other means of support, are forced into the labor market despite their preference for the role of Nurturer. Strivers are a group of self-motivated individuals who are not reluctant to participate in the workforce. Strivers ultimately, in fact, make welfare reform successful. The 1996 welfare reforms facilitate individual actions, especially for those who are predisposed to be self-sufficient. The reform only affects the Disaffected marginally, heightening their level of disorganization and their inability to contend with daily life. For the Disaffected, reforms solve few problems and amplify the dilemmas they face, which in the end remain unresolved.

Notes

2—Making the Words Flesh

1. Caseload figures reported by the Illinois Department of Public Aid and those reported by the U.S. Committee on Ways and Means in the <u>Green Book</u> differ somewhat, although the general trends are the same.

3—The Illinois Families Study

1. For more details on the IFS, see www.northwestern.edu/ipr/research/IFS.html.

2. Northwestern University received funding from the Searle Fund to conduct a qualitative supplement to the Illinois Families Study. The purpose of the qualitative component is to gain a deeper understanding of the process that families undergo as they move toward self-sufficiency. Specific areas of inquiry include work, identity, relationships, education, and child well-being. Research assistants began conducting the in-person qualitative interviews during the summer of 2000. The sample includes approximately 60 Chicago-area participants randomly selected from the Illinois Families Study.

3. To adjust for attrition between surveys, we used the same method in 2003 as that used to adjust for nonreponse in prior surveys (using administrative data from the original sampling frame, as well as a wide range of survey data from 2002). We applied these nonresponse adjustment weights, in conjunction with the base weights that correct for this stratification design, to the final 2003 sample, and we use these adjusted figures in all data analysis.

4—Two Worlds of Welfare

1. Committee on Ways and Means (2004). Section 13, p. 41. The $34 billion was a preliminary estimate.

2. Holt (2006).

3. Unlike several tax credits, the EITC is "refundable," which is especially helpful to low-income families. If a family owes income tax, the EITC reduces the tax liability by the amount of the EITC. If the person owed only $500 in taxes and was due an EITC of $4,500, he or she would receive a refund of $4,000. If the person owes no taxes, he

or she receives the full amount of EITC due. Refundability allows low-income workers who miss out on the benefits of most tax credits and deductions to take full advantage of the incentives in the EITC.

5—Working and Earning After Welfare Reform

1. We constructed a variable that represents the proportion of months that individuals worked during each period by dividing the number of months they worked within that period by its total number of months. In other words, we use a relative measure instead of an absolute measure of labor force participation. We also conducted sensitivity analyses using the absolute measure (the number of months a person worked) as the dependent variable, and our estimates were comparable to those produced from analyses using the relative measure.

2. We use repeated measures models with nested structure to include all information available from all four waves and determine changes in labor force participation or earnings over time. Such analyses are more likely to produce tests with higher statistical power, and thus there is a greater probability of detecting significant associations of interest.

3. We employ two-level hierarchical linear models that satisfy both conditions, that is, provide robust standard errors and allow for random effects of change over time (see Raudenbush and Bryk, 2002). At the first level, we use a temporal change model where an individual's development is portrayed by a "growth" trajectory that is unique for each individual. The first level is hence a within-person model with repeated observations for each person over time. At the second level, the growth over time becomes an outcome variable that is regressed on individual characteristics. The second-level model is therefore a between-person model. Specifically, at the first level we employ a linear change model. If we assume that there are t repeated observations over time for person i, then the first-level model is described as

$$Y_{ti} = \beta_{0i} + \beta_{1i} Wave_{ti} + \varepsilon_{ti'}$$

where Y_{ti} represents labor force participation or earnings for time t (wave 1 for example) for individual i; β_{0i} represents the initial status of labor force participation or earnings in wave 1; β_{1i} represents the temporal change in labor force participation or earnings from wave 1 to wave 4; and $\varepsilon_{ti'}$ is a wave- and person-specific residual.

At the second level, we predict temporal change using our wave 1 predictors, and thus our model is described as

$$\beta_{1i} = y_{10} + \sum_{q=1}^{Q} y_{1q} X_{qi} + u_{1i'}$$

where X_{qi} represents q person-specific predictors (e.g., race); y_{1q} represents the regression coefficients indicating the associations between temporal change and individuals' characteristics, respectively; y_{10} represents the average change over time; and u_{1i} is a person-specific residual, the variance of which indicates differences in change over time across individuals.

4. It is possible, although unlikely, that reverse causation is at work here. Although it may be the case that those who work more are more likely to be self-supporting and hence eligible to receive a rent voucher (such as Section 8), our measure of housing subsidies includes all forms of government support for rent, including public housing. It seem implausible that residents of public housing work more, so we argue that government support for rent affects labor force participation and not the other way around.

5. The relationship between initial income and growth in income observed in our data is in keeping with a pattern of regression to the mean that typically occurs

with unreliable, self-report measures. However, our confidence in the findings of a ceiling effect is bolstered by piecewise linear models (results not presented here), which allow the relationships between initial income growth to vary within each quartile of the income distribution. The piecewise linear models reinforce the finding of a ceiling effect, suggesting a negative, linear relationship between income growth and wave 1 income. Moreover, analysis of unemployment insurance records for the same sample and time period, which offer an administrative report of formal economic earnings (Sinha and Lewis, 2005), shows an almost identical pattern.

6—Depression and Welfare

1. Derr et al. (2000) suggest a number of reasons why no systematic effort exists. One reason is the challenge of integrating mental health and employment services, which typically exist in different government departments or agencies. Another reason is the reliance on employment case managers, who usually do not have appropriate tools or training to identify clients in need of mental health services.

2. Respondents had minimal work experience if they had worked fewer than 20 percent of the years since they turned 18; such a measure was established by Danziger et al., 2000a. They were considered to have few job skills if they had performed fewer than four of eight tasks on the job identified by Holzer (1996) as being related to employment success. These tasks included: talking with customers face-to-face or over the phone; reading instruction or reports; writing letters or memos; working with a computer; working with electronic machines; doing arithmetic or making change; filling out forms; and watching gauges or instruments.

3. To assess the extent to which our study participants received mental health services for depression, we used Medicaid paid claims. In other words, we identified those who received either outpatient or inpatient mental health services that were paid for by Medicaid at any time between January 1, 1998, and June 30, 1999. Claims for inpatient psychiatric hospitalization are selected according to the category of service on the claims records. Outpatient claims are identified by a combination of the category of service, procedure code, and International Classification of Disease version 9 — Clinical Modification (ICD-9-CM) primary diagnosis. Categories of service include psychiatric clinic services, Department of Mental Health and Developmental Disabilities (DMHDD) rehabilitation option services, and DMHDD targeted case management services. Both Current Procedural Terminology (CPT) and Healthcare Common Procedure Coding System (HCPCS) procedure codes are used to identify counseling and psychotherapy services. Finally, ICD-9-CM diagnosis codes were used to identify outpatient services that resulted in a diagnosis of a psychiatric condition. Diagnosis codes were first grouped into categories according to the Clinical Classifications Software (1999). From these broader groupings, affective disorders, schizophrenia, other psychoses, anxiety, pre-adult disorders, and other mental conditions were selected.

4. To study the independent effect of depression on employment among the welfare population, we used a five-step multivariate analysis. Model 1 includes demographic characteristics, Model 2 adds duration of welfare receipt, Model 3 includes domestic violence and the health status of the respondent and his/her children, and Model 4 adds human capital variables. We examine the effect of depression in Model 5, the "full" model that includes all covariates. The results for all covariates except for race-ethnicity, duration of welfare receipt, domestic violence, and education are consistent across models.

5. Other findings are not central to this study but are worth noting. In both study populations, Hispanics were more likely to be working than African Americans. There are several possible explanations for this result. Within the Illinois "work first" approach, it is up to recipients to find work on their own. Communities that are deeply

distressed or that have weak employment networks may create environments that limit work opportunities. African Americans, especially in Chicago, are vulnerable to this result. The stronger effect of race-ethnicity among the depressed subsample suggests that depression and work may have a stronger relationship among African Americans than among Hispanics. This may mean that discrimination along racial lines plays a role in limiting employment, although we cannot be sure without further investigation.

9—Did Welfare Reform Launch the Poor into Better Neighborhoods?

1. We compared them to 184 individuals who had dropped out of the study's Chicago sample on a broad range of background, employment, and income characteristics to ensure that the 403 individuals were no different in any meaningful way from others in the sample.

2. These self-reports of income are generally considered less reliable than administrative reports of earnings, such as unemployment insurance records, which were also available to us. However, they have the advantage of allowing respondents to include income from other household members, governmental assistance, activities in the informal economy, and other sources. Thus, they offer a more global measure of household resources than individual earnings records.

3. We conduct analyses using hierarchical linear models (HLM) that allow us to examine patterns in income and residential mobility. These models are designed to deal with a hierarchy (or nested structure) of the IFS longitudinal data by computing statistical analyses for multiple levels of data. The models presented here have two levels: For each individual, we have 3 observations of income or neighborhood demographic characteristics. Three observations of income or neighborhood characteristics are includd at level 1, and wave 1 individual characteristics are included at level 2. Initial analyses revealed little change in level 2 control variables across the three waves and little consistent effect of the changes that were found; therefore, we only control for wave 1 characteristics in the models presented in this paper. The level 1 model used in this analysis treats household income as the outcome and time as the independent variable, modeling the income growth over the three waves. The coefficient for time in this model represents income growth, or the change in income per one unit change in time (a one unit change in time is the movement from wave 1 to wave 2, or wave 2 to wave 3), and provides the answer to our first question. This measure of estimated income growth is the dependent variable at level 2. At level 2, we also control for the battery of wave 1 individual characteristics described above (age at first birth, number of children, age of children, education, work status, years of welfare receipt, years in residence, race, income, and housing assistance receipt). Thus, the level 2 equation examines the effect of wave 1 characteristics on the income growth observed across the three waves of IFS data.

Again, we use two level-HLM analyses with observations of neighborhood characteristics at time 1 and time 2 nested within individuals. At level 1, neighborhood demographic characteristics, such as the percentage of Black individuals, are outcome variables, and time (wave 1, wave 2, wave 3) is the independent variable. Thus, level 1 models the change in an individual's neighborhood characteristics over three waves.

4. In the Chicago metropolitan region, this reduction was offset by a 2 percent increase in poverty in the Cook County suburbs.

5. "Community" in this context means a "community area." Chicago has 77 community areas.

6. In particular, two community areas, Near West Side and Near South Side, saw a decrease of the African American population of more than 10 percentage points, while Chicago Lawn and Ashburn saw a greater than 10 percent increase in the African American population.

References

Abaya, Edwin. (Ed.) (1999). *Basics of Illinois welfare law: The Illinois TANF program and other related programs*. Chicago: Poverty Law Project of the National Clearinghouse for Legal Services.

Acs, G., & Loprest, P. J. (2001). *Initial synthesis report of the findings from ASPE's "Leavers" grants*. Washington, DC: Urban Institute.

Agency for Health Care Policy and Research. (1999). *Clinical Classifications Software (CCS) summary and downloading information*. Rockville, MD.

Allard, M. A., Albelda, R., Colten, M. E., & Cosenza, C. (1997). *In harm's way? Domestic violence, AFDC receipt, and welfare reform in Massachusetts*. Boston, MA: University of Massachusetts.

Allard, Scott W., & Danziger, Sheldon. (2003). "Proximity and opportunity: How residence and race affect the employment of welfare recipients." Housing Policy Debate 13(4): 675–700.

Alter, Catherine. (1996). "Family support as an intervention with female long-term AFDC recipients." *Social Work Research 20*, 203–16.

Amato, Paul R., & Sobolewski, Juliana M. (2001). "The effects of divorce and marital discord on adult children's psychological well-being." *American Sociological Review, 66*(6), 900–21.

American Enterprise Institute for Public Policy Research. (1994). *Welfare, marital status, and program overlap in Illinois*. Washington, DC.

Bandura, Albert. (1982). "Self-efficacy mechanism in human agency." *American Psychologist, 37*, 122–47.

Bandura, Albert. (1994). *Self-efficacy: The exercise of control*. New York: Freeman.

Becker, G. S. (1964). *Human capital*. New York: Columbia University Press.

Becker, G. S. (1966). Introduction. In C. Shaw (Ed.), *The Jack-roller*. Chicago: University of Chicago Press.

Benjamin, Lois, & James Stewart. (1989). "The self-concept of Black and White women: The influences upon its formation of welfare dependency, work effort, family networks, and illnesses." *American Journal of Economics and Sociology, 48*, 165–75.

Blank, R. (2002). "Evaluating welfare reform in the United States." *Journal of Economic Literature, 40*(4): 1105–66.

Blank, R. (2007). *What we know, what we don't know, and what we need to know about welfare reform*. National Poverty Center Working Paper Series #07–19. Ann Arbor: National Poverty Center, University of Michigan.

Blank, Rebecca M. (1997). *It takes a nation: A new agenda for fighting poverty*. New York: Russell Sage Foundation.

Boardman, Jason D., & Robert, Stephanie A. (2000). "Neighborhood socioeconomic status and perceptions of self-efficacy." *Sociological Perspectives 43*, 117–36.

Bogenschneider, K. (1997). "Parental involvement in adolescent schooling: A proximal process with transcontextual validity." *Journal of Marriage and the Family, 59*, 718–33.

Born, C. E., Caudill, P. J., & Cordero, M. L. (1999). "Life after welfare: A look at sanctioned families." University of Maryland School of Social Work, Baltimore.

Bos, Hans, Huston, Aletha, Granger, Robert, Duncan, Greg, Brock, Tom, & McLoyd, Vonnie. (1999). *New hope for people with low incomes: Two-year results of a program to reduce poverty and reform welfare*. New York: MDRC.

Brandwein, R. A. (1999). Family violence, women, and welfare. In R. A. Brandwein (Ed.), *Women, children, and welfare reform: The ties that bind*. Thousand Oaks, CA: Sage Publications.

Brauner, S., & Loprest, P. J. (1999). *Where are they now? What states' studies of people who left welfare tell us*. Washington, DC: The Urban Institute, No. A-32.

Brooks-Gunn, J., & Duncan, G. J. (1997). The effects of poverty on children. *Future of Children, 7*, 55–71.

Bureau of Economic and Business Research. (1989–1993). *Illinois statistical abstract*. Champaign, IL: University of Illinois at Urbana-Champaign.

Burkhauser, R. V., & Daly, M. C. (1996). "Employment and economic well-being following the onset of a disability: The role for public policy." In J. Mashaw et al. (Eds.), *Disability, work and cash benefits*. Kalamazoo, MI: Upjohn Institute for Employment Research.

Cancian, M., & Meyer, D. R. (2000). "Work after welfare: Women's work effort, occupation, and economic well-being." *Social Work Research, 24*(2), 69–86.

Cancian, Maria, Haveman, Robert H., & Wolfe, Barbara. (2002, December). "Before and after TANF: The economic well-being of women leaving welfare." *Social Service Review*, 603–41.

Canter, D. (1994). *Criminal shadows*. London: Harper Collins.

Chase-Lansdale, P. Lindsay, Moffitt, Robert A., Lohman, Brenda J., Cherlin, Andrew J., & Coley, Rebekah Levine, et al. (2003). "Mothers' transitions from welfare to work and the well-being of preschoolers and adolescents." *Science, 299*(5612), 1548–52.

Cherlin, A., Bogen, K., Quane, J. M., & Burton, L. (2002). "Operating within the rules: Welfare recipients' experiences with sanctions and case closings." *Social Service Review, 76*(3), 387–405.

Chicago Housing Authority. (2000). Plan for transformation.

Collins, A., & Aber, J. L. (1997). *How welfare reform can help or hurt children*. New York, NY: National Center for Children in Poverty.

Committee on Ways and Means, U.S. House of Representatives. (1994). *Overview of entitlement programs* (1994 Green Book). Washington, DC.

Cunningham, K., Wolbert, R., & Brockmeier, M. B. (2000). "Moving beyond the illness: Factors contributing to gaining and maintaining employment." *American Journal of Community Psychology, 28*(4), 481–94.

Currie, E. (1993). "Shifting the balance: On social action and the future of criminological research. *Journal of Research in Crime and Delinquency, 30*, 426–44.

Curry, Lewis, Snyder, C. R., Cook, David, Ruby, Brent, & Rehm, Michael. (1997). "Role of hope in academic and sport achievement." *Journal of Personality and Social Psychology, 73*, 1257–67.

Danziger, S. K., Corcoran, M. K., Danziger, S. H., Heflin, C., Kalil, A., Levine, J., et al. (2000). "Barriers to the employment of welfare recipients." In R. Cherry & W. M. Rodgers III (Eds.), *Prosperity for all? The economic boom and African Americans*. New York: Russell Sage Foundation.

Danziger, Sheldon, Haveman, Robert, & Plotnick, Robert. (1981). "How income transfers affect work, savings, and the income distribution: A critical review." *Journal of Economic Literature 19*(3), 975–1028.

Danziger, Sheldon, Heflin, Colleen M., Corcoran, Mary E., Oltmans, Elizabeth, & Wang, Hui-Chen. (2002). *Does it pay to move from welfare to work?* Ann Arbor, MI: Poverty Research and Training Center, University of Michigan.

Danziger, S. K., Kalil, A., & Anderson, N. J. (2000). "Human capital, health and mental health of welfare recipients: Co-occurrence and correlates." *Journal of Social Issues, 54*(4), 637–56.

Derr, M. K., Hill, H., & Pavetti, L. (2000). *Addressing mental health problems among TANF recipients: A guide for program administrators.* Washington, DC: Mathematic Policy Research Institute.

Devins, G. M., & Orme, C. M. (1984). "Center for Epidemiological Studies Depression scale." *Test Critiques,* 144–60.

Dewa, C. S., & Lin, E. (2000). "Chronic physical illness, psychiatric disorder and disability in the workplace." *Social Science and Medicine, 51,* 41–50.

Dooley, D., Prause, J., & Ham-Rowbottom, K. A. (2000). "Underemployment and depression: Longitudinal relationships." *Journal of Health and Social Behavior, 41*(41), 421–36.

Duncan, Greg J., & Caspary, Gretchen. (1997). "Welfare dynamics and the 1996 welfare reform." *Notre Dame Journal of Law,* 605–32.

Duncan, Greg J., & Chase-Lansdale, P. L. (2001). "Welfare reform and child well-being." In R. B. Blank & R. T. Haskins (Eds.), *The new world of welfare.* Washington, DC: Brookings Institution Press, 391–417.

Duncan, Greg J., Dunifon, Rachel E., Doran, Morgan B. Ward, & Yeung, W. Jean. (2001). "How different are welfare and working families? And do these differences matter for children's achievement?" In Greg Duncan & P. Lindsay Chase-Landsdale (Eds.), *For better and for worse: Welfare reform and the well-being of children and families.* New York: Russell Sage Foundation, 103–31.

Duncan, G., Huston, A. C., & Weisner, T. S. (2007). *Higher ground: New hope for the working poor and their children.* New York: Russell Sage Foundation.

Duncan, Greg J., Yeung, W. J., Brooks-Gunn, J., & Smith, J. R. (1998). "How much does childhood poverty affect the life chances of children?" *American Sociological Review 63,* 406–423.

Eckstein, H. (1992). "Civic inclusion and its discontents." *Regarding Politics: Essays on Political Theory, Stability, and Change.* Berkeley, University of California Press.

Edelhoch, M., Liu, Q., & Martin, L. (2000). "The post-welfare progress of sanctioned clients in South Carolina." *Journal of Applied Social Sciences 24*(2).

Edelman, P. (1997). "The worst thing Bill Clinton has done." *The Atlantic Monthly, 279*(3), 43–58.

Edin, Kathryn, & Lein, Laura. (1997). *Making ends meet: How single mothers survive welfare and low-wage work.* New York: Russell Sage Foundation.

Elazar, D. (1984). *American Federalism: A View from the States.* New York: Harper and Row.

Ellwood, D. (1988). *Poor support: Poverty in the American family.* New York: Basic Books.

Epstein, J. L. (2001). *Schools, family, and community partnerships: Preparing educators and improving schools.* Boulder, CO: Westview Press.

Erickson, Richard, Post, Robin, & Paige, Albert. (1975). "Hope as a psychiatric variable." *Journal of Clinical Psychology, 31,* 324–30.

Ferraro, Kenneth F. (1995). *Fear of crime: Interpreting victimization risk.* Albany: State University of New York Press.

Freedman, Steven, Friedlander, Daniel, & Riccio, James. (1993). *GAIN: Benefits, costs, and three-year impacts of a welfare-to-work program.* New York: MDRC.

Friedlander, D., Freedman, S., Hamilton, G., & Quint, J. (1987). *Illinois: The demonstration of state work/welfare initiatives: Final report on job search and work experience in Cook*

County. Report of the Manpower Demonstration Research Corporation. New York: Manpower Demonstration Research Corporation.

Furstenberg, Frank. (1971). "Public reaction to crime in the streets." *American Scholar, 40*, 601–10.

Gecas, Viktor. 1989. "The social psychology of self-efficacy." *Annual Review of Sociology, 15*, 291–316.

Goerge, R., & Lee, B. J. (2001). "Matching and cleaning administrative data." In C. F. Citro, R. Moffitt, & M. Ver Ploeg (Eds.), *Data collection and research issues for studies of welfare population: Panel on data and methods for measuring the effects of changes in social welfare programs*. Washington, DC: National Academy Press.

Goffman, E. (1961). *Asylums*. New York: Doubleday.

Gottschalk, Louis. (1974). "A hope scale applicable to verbal samples." *Archives of General Psychiatry, 30*, 779–85.

Gottschalk, Louis. (1985.) "Hope and other deterrents to illness." *American Journal of Psychotherapy, 39*, 515–24.

Gottschalk, Peter, McLanahan, Sara, & Sandefur, Gary. (1996). "The dynamics and intergenerational transmission of poverty and welfare participation." In Sheldon Danziger, Gary Sandefur, & Daniel Weinberg (Eds.), *Confronting poverty: Prescriptions for change*. Cambridge, MA: Harvard University Press, 85–108.

Griffin, J. M., Fuhrer, R., Stansfeld, S. A., & Marmot, M. (2002). "The importance of low control at work and home on depression and anxiety: Do these effects vary by gender and social class?" *Social Science & Medicine, 54*, 783–98.

Grogger, Jeffrey, & Karoly, Lynn. (2005). *Welfare reform: Effects of a decade of change*. Cambridge, MA: Harvard University Press.

Groves, W. B., & Lynch, M. J. (1990). "Reconciling structural and subjective approaches to the study of crime." *Journal of Research in Crime and Delinquency, 27*, 348–75.

Guo, G. (1998). "The timing of the influences of cumulative poverty on children's cognitive ability and achievement." *Social Forces, 77*, 257–87.

Hamilton, G., Brock, T., Farrell, M., Friedlander, D., & Harknett, K. (1997). *Evaluating two welfare-work approaches: Two-year findings on the labor force attachment and human capital development programs in three sites*. Washington, DC: Department of Health and Human Services, Administration for Children and Families and Assistant Secretary for Planning and Evaluation.

Handler, J. F., & Hasenfeld, Y. (1991). *The moral construction of poverty: Welfare reform in America*. Newbury Park, CA: Sage.

Harris, K. M., Boisjoly, J., & Duncan, G. J. (1997). *Time limits and welfare reform: New estimates of the number and characteristics of affected families*. Chicago: Joint Center for Poverty Research.

Hastings, Julia, Taylor, Sarah, & Austin, Michael J. (2006). "The status of low-income families in the post-welfare reform environment: Mapping the relationships between poverty and family." *Journal of Health & Social Policy, 0897-7186, 21*(1), 33–63.

Henderson, A. T., & Berla, N. (1994). *A new generation of evidence: The family is critical to student achievement*. Washington, DC: National Committee for Citizens in Education.

Heneghan, A. M., Silver, E. J., Bauman, L. J., Westbrook, L. E., & Stein, R. E. K. (1998). "Depressive symptoms in inner-city mothers of young children: Who is at risk?" *Pediatrics, 102*(6), 1394–1400.

Herr, T., & Halpern, R. (1991). *Changing what counts: Rethinking the journey out of welfare*. Chicago: Erikson Institute.

Herr, T., & Halpern, R. (1993). *Bridging the worlds of Head Start and Welfare-to-Work: Building a two-generation self-sufficiency program from the ground up*. (Working paper). Chicago: Erikson Institute.

Herr, T., & Halpern, R. (1994). *Lessons from Project Match for welfare reform.* Chicago: Erikson Institute.

Hirsch, A. R. (1983). *Making the second ghetto: Race and housing in Chicago 1940–1960.* New York: Cambridge University Press.

Hofferth, S., Stanhope, S., & Harris, K. M. (2000). *Exiting welfare in the 1990s: Did public policy influence recipients' behavior?* Ann Arbor, MI: Population Studies Center at the Institute for Social Research, University of Michigan.

Holt, Steve. (2006). *The Earned Income Tax Credit at 30: What we know.* Washington, DC: Brookings Institution.

Holzer, H. (1996). *What employers want: Job prospects for less-educated workers.* New York: Russell Sage Foundation.

Hoover-Dempsey, K. V., & Sandler, H. M. (1995). "Parental involvement in children's education: Why does it make a difference?" *Teachers College Record, 97,* 310–31.

Huston, A. C., Duncan, G. J., Granger, R., Bos, J., McLoyd, V., Mistry, R., et al. (2001). "Work-based antipoverty programs for parents can enhance the school performance and social behavior of children." *Child Development, 72,* 318–36.

Illinois Department of Employment Security. (1995). *Illinois employment: Industry summary 1978–1994.* Chicago.

Illinois Department of Public Aid. (1986). *Project Chance annual status report.* Springfield, IL.

Illinois Department of Public Aid. (1987). *Project Chance: Report to General Assembly.* Fiscal year 1987. Springfield, IL.

Illinois Department of Public Aid. (1989). *Avenues toward self-sufficiency. Project Chance.* Fiscal year 1989. Springfield, IL.

Illinois Department of Public Aid. (1991). *Project Chance annual report.* Fiscal year 1991. Springfield, IL: Author.

Illinois Department of Public Aid. (1992). *Project Chance annual report.* Fiscal year 1992. Springfield, IL.

Illinois Department of Public Aid. (1993). *Welfare to work employment and training programs.* Annual Report, 1993. Springfield, IL.

Illinois Department of Public Aid. (1994). *Welfare to work employment and training programs.* Annual Report, 1993. Springfield, IL.

Illinois Department of Public Aid—Systems Development Section. (1995). *AFDC and Food Stamp Allotments.* Unpublished raw data.

Illinois General Assembly. (1997). *Temporary assistance for needy families.* Illinois Public Aid Code (305 ILCS 5/Article IV).

Illinois Tax Foundation. (1995). *Pocket guide to the Illinois state budget.* Springfield, IL.

Izzo, C. V., Weissber, R. P., & Kasprow, W. J. (1999). "A longitudinal assessment of teacher perceptions of parent involvement in children's education and school performance." *American Journal of Community Psychology, 27,* 817–39.

Jackson, Aurora. (2000). "Maternal self-efficacy and children's influence on stress and parenting among single black mothers in poverty." *Journal of Family Issues, 21,* 3–16.

Jargowsky, P. (1996). "Take the money and run: Economic segregation in U.S. metropolitan areas." *American Sociological Review, 61*(6), 984–98.

Jargowsky, P. (2003). "Stunning progress, hidden problems: The dramatic decline of concentrated poverty in the 1990s." Washington, DC: Center on Urban and Metropolitan Policy, the Brookings Institution.

Jargowsky, P., & Sawhill, I. V. (2006). *The decline of the underclass.* Policy Brief # 36. Washington, DC: The Brookings Institution.

Jaro, M. A. (1985). Current Record Linkage Research. *Proceedings of the Statistical Computing Section, American Statistical Association,* 140–43.

Jaro, M. A. (1989). "Advances in record-linkage methodology as applied to matching the 1985 census of Tampa, Florida." *Journal of the American Statistical Association,* 84(406), 414–20.

Jarrett, Robin. (1996). "Welfare stigma among low-income African American single mothers." *Family Relations, 45,* 368–74.

Jayakody, R., Danziger, S., & Pollack, H. (2000). "Welfare reform, substance use, and mental health." *Journal of Health Politics, Policy, and Law, 25*(4), 623–51.

Jayakody, R., & Stauffer, D. (2000). "Mental health problems among single mothers: Implications for work and welfare reform." *Journal of Social Issues, 56*(4), 617–34.

Kalil, A., Seefeldt, K. S., & Wang, H. (2002). "Sanctions and material hardship under TANF." *Social Service Review, 76*(4), 642–62.

Kane, Thomas J. (1987). "Giving back control: Long-term poverty and motivation." *Social Service Review, 61,* 405–19.

Katz, J. (1988). *Seductions of crime: The moral and sensual attractions of doing evil.* New York: Basic Books.

Kessler, R. C. (1997). "The effects of stressful life events on depression." *Annual Review of Psychology, 48,* 191–214.

Kessler, R. C., Berglund, P., Demler, O., Jin, R., Koretz, D., Merikangas, K. R., et al. (2003). "The epidemiology of Major Depressive Disorder: Results from the National Comorbidity Survey Replication (NCS-R)." *Journal of the American Medical Association, 289,* 3095–3105.

Kingsley, G. T., & Pettit, K. L. S. (2003, May). *Concentrated poverty: A change in course. Neighborhood change in urban America.* No. 2. Washington, DC: The Urban Institute.

Klawitter, Marieka, Plotnick, Robert, & Edwards, Mark Evan. (2000). "Determinants of initial entry onto welfare by young women." *Journal of Policy Analysis and Management, 19,* 527–46.

Korenman, Sanders, & Neumark, David. (1991). "Does marriage really make men more productive?" *Journal of Human Resources, 26*(2), 282–307.

Kunz, James, & Kalil, Ariel. (1999)."Self-esteem, self-efficacy, and welfare use." *Social Work Research, 23,* 119–26.

Lazarus, A. A. (1980). "Toward delineating some causes of change in psychotherapy." *Professional Psychology, 11,* 863–70.

Lareau, A. (1989). *Home advantage: Social class and parental intervention in elementary education.* London: Falmer.

Lee, Bong Joo, Goerge, R., & Dilts, J. (2000). *Outcomes for the income maintenance caseload during receipt: Caseload dynamics, employment, and earnings in Illinois, 1991–1999.* Discussion paper. Chicago: Chapin Hall Center for Children.

Lehrer, E., Crittenden, K, & Noor, K. F. (2002). "Depression and economic self-sufficiency among inner-city minority mothers." *Social Science Research, 31*(3), 285–309.

Leuchtenburg, William Edward. (1963). *Franklin D. Roosevelt and the New Deal, 1932–1940* (1st ed.). New York: Harper & Row.

Lewis, D. A. (1990). "From programs to lives: A comment." *American Journal of Community Psychology, 18,* 923–26.

Lewis, D. A., Amsden, L. B., Slack, K. S., & Lee, B. J. (2002). *Welfare reform in Illinois: Is the moderate approach working?* Evanston, IL: Institute for Policy Research, Northwestern University.

Lewis, D. A., Amsden, L. B., Slack, K. S., & Lee, B. J. (2004). "The two worlds of welfare reform in Illinois: Work and welfare six years after reform." Evanston, IL: Institute for Policy Research, Northwestern University.

Lewis, D. A., & Maruna, S. (1998). "Person-centered policy analysis." *Research in Public Policy and Management, 9,* 213–30.

Lewis, D. A., Riger, S., Rosenberg, H., Wagenaar, H., Lurigio, A. J., & Reed, S. (1991). *Worlds of the mentally ill: How deinstitutionalization works in the city.* Carbondale, IL: Southern Illinois University Press.

Lewis, D. A., Shadish, W. R., & Lurigio, A. J. (1989). "Policies of inclusion and the mentally ill: Long-term care in a new environment." *Journal of Social Issues, 45*(3), 173–86.

Lewis, D. A., et al. (2000, November). *Work, welfare, and well-being: An independent look at welfare reform in Illinois.* Evanston, IL: Institute for Policy Research, Northwestern University.

Lewis, Dan A., George, Christine, George, & Puntenney, Deborah. (1999). "Welfare reform efforts in Illinois." In Lawrence Joseph (Ed.), *Families, poverty, and welfare reform: Confronting a New Policy Era* (99–138). Chicago: University of Chicago.

Lewis, J., Riger, S., & Goerge, R. (2003). *Preserving the gains, rethinking the losses: Welfare in Illinois five years after reform. Third annual report of the Illinois Families Study.* Evanston, IL: Institute for Policy Research.

Lohman, B. J., Pittman, L. D., Coley, R. L., Chase-Lansdale, P. L. (2004). "Welfare history, sanctions, and developmental outcomes among low-income children and youth." *Social Service Review, 78,* 41–73.

Magaletta, Philip, & Oliver, J. M. (1999). "The hope construct, will, and ways: Their relations with self-efficacy, optimism, and general well-being." *Journal of Clinical Psychology, 55,* 539–51.

Maltz, M. (1994). Deviating from the mean: The declining significance of significance. *Journal of Research in Crime and Delinquency, 31,* 434–463.

Mancuso, D. C., & Lindler, V. L. (2001). *Examining the circumstances of welfare leavers and sanctioned families in Sonoma County: Final report.* Burlingame, CA: SPHERE Institute.

Maruna, S. (1995). *Criminology, desistance, and the psychology of the stranger.* Paper presented at the 1995 American Society of Criminology conference, Boston, MA.

Massey, D. S., Condran, G. A., & Denton, N. A. (1987). "The effect of residential segregation on black social and economic well-being." *Social Forces, 66*(1), 29–56.

Massey, D. S., & Denton, N. A. (1989). "Hypersegregation in U.S. metropolitan areas: Black and Hispanic segregation along five dimensions." *Demography, 26*(3), 373–91.

Massey, D. S., & Denton, N. A. (1993). *American Apartheid: Segregation and the making of the underclass.* Cambridge, MA: Harvard University Press.

Massey, D. S., & Fischer, M. J. (2000). "How segregation concentrates poverty." *Ethnic and Racial Studies, 23*(4), 670–91.

Maynard, Rebecca. (1997). *Kids having kids.* Washington, DC: Urban Institute.

McCord, J. (1990). "Problem behaviors." In S. S. Feldman & G. R. Elliot (Eds.), *At the threshold: The developing adolescent.* Cambridge, MA: Harvard University Press.

Mead, L. (2004). *Government matters: Welfare reform in Wisconsin.* Princeton: Princeton University Press.

Mead, Lawrence M. (1986). *Beyond entitlement: The social obligations of citizenship.* New York: Free Press.

Menaghan, E. G., & Parcel, T. L. (1995). "Social sources of change in children's home environments: The effects of parental occupational experiences and family conditions." *Journal of Marriage and the Family, 57,* 69–84.

Menand, Louis. (1997). *Pragmatism: A reader.* New York: Vintage.

Michalopoulos, C., Schwartz, C., & Adams-Ciardullo, D. (2000). *National evaluation of welfare-to-work strategies: What works best for whom. Impacts of 20 welfare-to-work programs by subgroup.* New York: Manpower Demonstration Research Corporation.

Moffit, Robert. (1992). "Incentive effects of the U.S. welfare system: A review." *Journal of Economic Literature, 30,* 1–61.

Moffitt, T. E. (1993). "Adolescence-limited and life-course-persistent antisocial behavior: A developmental taxonomy." *Psychological Review, 100,* 674–701.

Moore, K. M., & Driscoll, A. K. (1997). "Low-wage maternal employment and outcomes for children: A study." *The Future of Children, 7,* 122–127.

Morris, P. A., Huston, A. C., Duncan, G. J., Crosby, D. A., & Bos, J. M. (2001). *How welfare and work policies affect children: A synthesis of research.* New York: Manpower Demonstration Research Corporation.

Murray, C. (1984). *Losing ground: American social policy, 1950–1980.* New York: Basic Books.

National Governor's Conference. (1969). *Welfare reform.* Resolution adopted at the 61st Annual Meeting of the National Governor's Conference, Colorado Springs.

Nelson, B. (1990). The origins of the two-channel welfare state: Workman's compensation and mother's aid. In L. Gordon (Ed.), *Women, the state, and welfare.* Madison, WI: University of Wisconsin Press, 123–51.

Newcombe, H. B. (1988). *Handbook of record linkage: Methods for health and statistical studies, administration, and business.* Oxford: Oxford University Press.

Nichols, Austin. (2006, August). *Understanding recent changes in child poverty.* (New Federalism issue brief.) Washington, DC: Urban Institute.

Nixon, R. (1969, December 5). "Address to the White House Conference on Food, Nutrition, and Health, Dec. 2, 1969." *Congressional Quarterly Weekly Report,* 2515–16.

O'Connor, A. (2001). *Poverty knowledge: Social science, social policy, and the poor in twentieth-century U.S. history.* Princeton: Princeton University Press.

Olson, K., & Pavetti, L. (1996). *Personal and family challenges to the successful transition from welfare to work.* Washington, DC: The Urban Institute.

O'Neill, June. (1990). "The role of human capital in earnings differences between black and white men." *Journal of Economic Perspectives 4,* 25–46.

Parcel, T. L., & Menaghan, E. G. (1994). "Early parental work, family social capital, and early-childhood outcomes." *American Journal of Sociology, 99,* 972–1009.

Parcel, T. L., & Menaghan, E. G. (1997). "Effects of low-wage employment on family well-being." *The Future of Children, 7,* 116–21.

Park, R. (1936). "Human Ecology." *American Journal of Sociology, 42,* 1–15.

Park, R., & Burgess, E. (1925). *The city.* Chicago: University of Chicago Press.

Parker, Louise. (1994). "The role of workplace support in facilitating self-sufficiency among single mothers on welfare." *Family Relations, 43,* 168–73.

Petterson, S. M., & Albers, A. B. (2001). "Effects of poverty and maternal depression on early child development." *Child Development, 72,* 1794–1813.

Pavetti, L., Derr, M. K., & Hesketh, H. (2003). *Review of sanction policies and research studies: Final literature review.* Report to the Department of Health and Human Services, Office of the Assistant Secretary for Planning and Evaluation. Washington, DC: Mathematica Policy Research, Inc.

Pavetti, L., & Wemmerus, N. (1999). "From a welfare check to a paycheck: Creating a new social contract." *Journal of Labor Research. 20*(4), 517–37.

Pearlin, Leonard, & Schooler, Carmi. (1978). "The structure of coping." *Journal of Health and Social Behavior, 19,* 2–21.

The Personal Responsibility and Work Opportunity Reconciliation Act of 1996. (2006) Retrieved May 4, 2006, from http://www.acf.dhhs.gov/programs/ofa/prwora96.htm.

Pervin, Lawrence A. (1989). *Goal concepts in personality and social psychology.* Hillsdale, NJ: L. Erlbaum Associates.

Petterson, Stephen M., & Friel, Lisa V. (2001). "Psychological distress, hopelessness and welfare." *Women & Health 32,* 79–99.

Polit, D. F., London, A. S., & Martinez, J. M. (2001). *The health of poor urban women: Findings from the Project on Devolution and Urban Change.* New York: Manpower Demonstration Research Corporation.

Popkin, Susan. (1990). "Welfare: Views from the bottom." *Social Problems 37,* 64–78.

Quint, J. C., Bos, J. M., & Polit, D. F. (1997). *New chance: Final report on a comprehensive program for young mothers in poverty and their children.* New York: Manpower Demonstration Research Corporation.

Radloff, L. S. (1977). "The CES-D scale: A self-report depression scale for research in the general population." *Applied Psychological Measurement, 1*, 385–401.

Rainwater, L. (1970). *Behind ghetto walls: Black families in a federal slum*. Chicago: Aldine.

Raudenbush, Steven W., & Bryk, Anthony S. (2002). *Hierarchical linear models: Applications and data analysis methods*. Newbury Park: Sage.

Rector, R. E., & Youssef, S. E. (1999). *The determinants of welfare caseload decline*. Washington, DC: Heritage Foundation.

Rolston, H. (1999). *Effects of changes to the welfare system. Testimony before the Subcommittee on Human Resources of the House Committee on Ways and Means*.

Ross, C. E., Mirowsky, J., & Huber, J. (1983). "Dividing work, sharing work, and in between: Marriage patterns and depression." *American Sociological Review, 48*, 809–23.

Rossi, P. H., Berk, R. A., & Lenihan, K. J. (1980). *Money, work, and crime*. New York: Academic Press.

Sampson, R. J. (1993). "Linking time and place: Dynamic contextualism and the future of criminological inquiry." *Journal of Research in Crime and Delinquency, 30*, 426–44.

Sampson, R. J., & Laub, J. (1992). "Crime and deviance in the life course." *Annual Review of Sociology, 18*, 63–84.

Sampson, R. J., & Laub, J. (1993). *Crime in the making: Pathways and turning points through life*. Cambridge, MA: Harvard University Press.

Schlesinger, A. (1959). *The coming of the New Deal*. Boston: Houghton Mifflin.

Scott, Ellen K., Edin, Kathryn, London, Andrew S., & Mazelis, Joan Maya. (2001). "My children come first: Welfare-reliant women's post TANF views of work-family trade-offs and marriage." In Greg Duncan & P. Lindsay Chase-Landsdale (Eds.), *For better and for worse: Welfare reform and the well-being of children and families* (132–53). New York: Russell Sage Foundation.

Scott, M. B., & Lyman, S. M. (1968). "Accounts." *American Sociological Review, 33*, 46–61.

Secret, M., & Peck-Heath, C. (2004). "Maternal labor force participation and child well-being in public assistance families." *Journal of Family Issues, 25*, 520–41.

Seeman, M. (1991). "Alienation and anomie." In J. P. Robinson, P. R. Shaver, & L. S. Wrightsman (Eds.), *Measures of Personality and Social Psychological Attitudes* (291–372). San Diego: Academic Press.

Segal, Elizabeth A. (1997). "Welfare reform and the myth of the marketplace." *Journal of Poverty, 1*, 5–18.

Shaw, C. (1929). *Delinquency areas*. Chicago: University of Chicago Press.

Shaw, C. (1930). *The jack-roller: A delinquent boy's own story*. Chicago: University of Chicago Press.

Shelley v. Kraemer 334 U.S. 1 (1948).

Shook, K. (1999). *Does the loss of welfare income increase the risk of child welfare involvement among families receiving welfare?* Ann Arbor, MI: UMI Dissertation Services.

Siegal, G., & Loman, L. (1991). *Child care and AFDC recipients in Illinois: Patterns, problems, and needs*. St. Louis, MO: Institute of Applied Research.

Sinha, V., & D. A. Lewis. (2005). *Earning and incomes of Illinios TANF recipients*. Paper presented at Society for the Study of Social Problems meeting, Philadelphia, PA.

Skocpol. T. (1992). *Protecting soldiers and mothers: The political origins of social policy in the United States*. Cambridge, MA: Harvard University Press.

Skocpol, T. (1995). *Social policy in the United States*. Princeton: Princeton University Press.

Smiley, Marion. (2001). "'Welfare dependence': The power of a concept." *Thesis Eleven, 64*, 21–38.

Smith, E. P., Atkins, J., & Connell, C. M. (2003). "Family, school, and community factors and relationships to racial-ethnic attitudes and academic achievement." *American Journal of Community Psychology, 32*, 159–73.

Smith, James, & Welch, Finis R. (1989, June). "Black economic progress after Myrdal." *Journal of Economic Literature, 27(2)*, 519–64.

Smith, J. R., Brooks-Gunn, J., Klebanov, P. K., & Lee, K. (2000). "Welfare and work: Complementary strategies for low-income women?" *Journal of Marriage and the Family, 62*, 808–21.

Snyder, C. R., ed. (2000). *Handbook of hope: Theory, measures, and applications.* San Diego, CA: Academic Press, Inc.

Snyder, C. R., Sympson, Susie, Ybasco, Florence, Borders, Tyrone, Babyak, Michael, & Higgins, Raymond. (1996). "Development and validation of the State Hope Scale." *Journal of Personality and Social Psychology, 70*, 321–35.

Snyder, C. R., Harris, Cheri, Anderson, John, Holleran, Sharon, Irving, Lori, Sigmon, Sandra, et al. (1991). "The will and the ways: Development and validation of an individual-differences measure of hope." *Journal of Personality and Social Psychology, 60*, 570–85.

Stack, C. B. (1974). *All our kin: Strategies for survival in a black community.* New York: Harper and Row.

Statistical Association, 84(406), 414–420.

Steinberg, L. D. (1996). *Beyond the classroom: Why school reform has failed and what parents need to do.* New York: Simon & Schuster.

Steiner, G. (1971). *The state of welfare.* Washington, DC: Brookings Institute.

Stricker, Frank. (2000). "Why American poverty rates stopped falling in the '70s, and why a better story was not told about it." *Journal of Poverty, 4*, 1–21.

Stueve, A., Dohrenwend, B. P., & Skodol, A. E. (1998). "Relationships between stressful life events and episodes of major depression and nonaffective psychotic disorders: Selected results from a New York risk factor study." *Adversity, Stress, and Psychopathology.* New York: Oxford University Press, 341–57.

SuiChu, E. H., & Willms, J. D. (1996). "Effects of parental involvement on eighth-grade achievement." *Sociology of Education, 69*, 126–41.

Sykes, G. M., & Matza, D. (1957). "Techniques of neutralization: A theory of delinquency." *American Sociological Review, 22*, 664–73.

Tausig, M. (1999). "Work and mental health." In C. S. Aneshensel & J. C. Phelan (Eds.), *Handbook of the sociology of mental health* (255–74). New York: Kluwer.

Taylor, Lorraine C. (2001). "Work attitudes, employment barriers, and mental health symptoms in a sample of rural welfare recipients." *American Journal of Community Psychology, 29*, 443–63.

Taylor, M. J., & Barusch, A. S. (2004). "Personal, family, and multiple barriers of long-term welfare recipients." *Social Work, 49(2)*, 175–83.

Tennant, C. (2002). "Life events, stress and depression: A review of the findings." *Australian and New Zealand Journal of Psychiatry, 36*, 173–82.

Thomas, W. I., & Znaneicki, F. (1919). *The Polish peasant in Europe and America.* Boston: Gotham Press.

Toch, H. (1987). "Supplementing the positivist approach." In M. Gotfredson & T. Hirschi (Eds.), *Positive criminology.* Beverly Hills, CA: Sage.

Todd, Janet L., & Worell, Judith. (2000). "Resilience in low-income, employed, African American women." *Psychology of Women Quarterly, 24*, 119–28.

Tolman, R., & Rosen, D. (2001). "Domestic violence in the lives of women receiving welfare: Mental health, substance dependence, and economic well-being." *Violence against Women, 7(2)*, 141–58.

Tweed, D. L. (1993). "Depression-related impairment: Estimating concurrent and lingering effects." *Psychological Medicine, 23*, 373–86.

U.S. Department of Health and Human Services. (1990, 1995, 2000–2002). *National vital statistics: Trends in characteristics of births by state, United States* (vol. 52, no. 19).

U.S. Department of Health and Human Services. (1995). *Vital statistics of the United States 1991, Volume 1–Natality.* Hyattsville, MD.

U.S. Department of Health and Human Services. (1999). *Mental health: A report of the surgeon general.* Rockville, MD: Substance Abuse and Mental Health Services Administration, Center for Mental Health Services, National Institutes of Health.

U.S. Department of Health and Human Services. (2001). *Mental health: Culture, race and ethnicity. A supplement to Mental health: A report of the surgeon general.* Rockville, MD: U.S. Public Health Service.

U.S. Department of Health and Human Services. (2007). *TANF families—Through December 2006* (table). Washington, DC: DHHS, Administration for Children and Families.

University Consortium on Welfare Reform. (2000). "Work, welfare, and well-being: An independent look at welfare reform in Illinois. Project description and first-year report."

Van Dongen, C. J. (1996). "Quality of life and self-esteem in working and nonworking persons with mental illness." *Community Mental Health Journal, 32*(6), 535–48.

Weaver, R. K. (2000). *Ending welfare as we know it: Policy making for low-income families in the United States.* Washington, DC: Brookings Institution.

Wilson, W. J. (1987). *The truly disadvantaged.* Chicago: University of Chicago Press.

Wilson, William J. (1996). *When work disappears: The world of the new urban poor* (1st ed.). New York: Knopf. Distributed by Random House, Inc.

Wirth, L. (1928). *The ghetto.* Chicago: University of Chicago Press.

Zaslow, M. J., & Emig, C. A. (1997). "When low-income mothers go to work: Implications for children." *The Future of Children, 7,* 110–15.

Zaslow, M. J., Moore, K. A., Brooks, J. L., Morris, P. A., Tout, K., Redd, Z. A., et al. (2002). "Experimental studies of welfare reform and children." *The Future of Children, 12,* 79–95.

Zedlewski, S. R. (1999). *Work activity and obstacles to work among TANF recipients.* Washington, DC: The Urban Institute.

Zellman, G. L., & Waterman, J. (1998). "Understanding the impact of parent school involvement on children's educational outcomes." *The Journal of Educational Research, 91,* 370–80.

Index

AFDC. See Aid to Families with Dependent Children (AFDC)

African-Americans: analysis of poor, 9; Chicago Public Housing Authority projects and, 115; concentrated poverty and, 112–113, 114; decline in poverty and, 117; depression and unemployed, 83; poverty and, 24, 25 table 2.1, 110, 111; poverty levels of, 118 and table 9.1; single mothers and, 16; teen birth rates and, 23, 24

Aid to Dependent Children. See Aid to Families with Dependent Children (AFDC)

Aid to Families with Dependent Children (AFDC): advantages and disadvantages of, 125, 126; cash assistance and, 15; decline in public assistance and, 25; decline of welfare caseloads and, 49; elimination of, 28, 29; expenditures by Midwestern states, 27 and table 2.3; expenditures of, 26 and table 2.2; race and percentage distribution of, 25 table 2.1; recipients, 1965-1996, 24 fig. 2.2; welfare and, 6

Birth rates: of teens and unmarried women, 23, 24

Carter, Jimmy, 16

Center for Epidemiological Studies Depression Scale (CES-D), 79

Chapin Hall Center for Children, 49

child care: benefits of, 90; labor force participation and, 75; type of, 57 fig. 4.2; welfare reform and, 56

children: academic achievement of, 90, 91; education and, 89; negative outcomes and, 88; welfare theories and, 87; work requirements of parents and, 89

Clinton, William J.: PRWORA and, 6; welfare reform and, 16

conservatives: AFDC and, 7; causes of poverty and, 114, 115; children and theories of, 87; context of competing paradigms, 126 fig. 10.2, 128; PRWORA effects and, 111; sanctions and, 109; welfare and, 9; welfare reform and, 8, 123, 124 and fig. 10.1

Contract with America movement: conservatives and, 30; House of Representative Republicans and, 16

del Valle, Miguel, 31

Democrats: Illinois welfare reform and, 30–32

demographic characteristics, 36 table 3.1, 37, 64 table 4.2, 67

depression: "reason to keep going" and, 85; factors of, 78, 79; human capital and, 82, 85–86; importance of work and, 84, 85; stress and, 77; welfare recipients and symptoms of, 83 and table 6.3

Earned Income Tax Credit (EITC): antipoverty program and, 20; Illinois work-related support and, 20; poverty rate and, 56, 57; work participation and, 52

education: children and achievement in, 90, 91; welfare recipients and, 89

Ellwood, David: liberal answer and, 17, 18
employment: categories of, 67, 68, 69
   table 5.1; human capital and, 66, 74;
   impact of stability, 88, 89; situational
   impact of, 90. *See also* work
Externalizing Problems from the Social
   Skills Rating System, 91

Family Support Act, 19, 28
Federal welfare policy: impact of, 21

Gingrich, Newt, 20

Hispanics: birth rates and, 23, 24;
   depression and employed, 83; high
   earnings and, 104
human capital: depression and, 82,
   85–86; employment and, 66, 74; high
   earnings and, 104

identity theorists, 11
Illinois Families Study (IFS): analysis of,
   37, 38; attitude and types in, 54, 55;
   caseload trends and, 53; Chicago
   and, 37; Chicago respondents and,
   115–116; Chicago welfare recipients
   and neighborhoods, 120–122; child
   care and, 55–56, 57 fig. 4.2; children
   and, 87–93; comparison of recipients,
   136 table 2; composition of, 135 table
   1; demographic characteristics of, 64
   table 4.2; depression symptoms and,
   79, 80 table 6.1; disaffected and, 43–45,
   136, 137; goal of, 34; health and well-
   being during, 59, 63; impediments to
   work and, 79; income growth and, 73,
   74, 75 table 5.5; mental health service
   use and, 81 and table 6.2; nurturers
   and, 38–39, 40, 53, 136, 137; panel
   study and, 14; person-centered policy
   analysis, 133; poverty levels and, 75,
   76; providers and, 40–42, 43, 50, 54,
   58, 136, 137; random samplings and
   five year study, 34–37; respondents'
   demographic characteristics and, 36
   table 3.1, 37; sanctioned respondents
   and, 99 and table 8.1; sanctions and,
   98; segregation and, 113; strivers and,
   50; types of recipients, 35, 38;
   vulnerable groups of, 61, 62 and fig.
   4.4, 63; welfare case study, 22, 50–52
Illinois General Assembly: TANF plan
   and, 20

Illinois welfare reform: "stopped clock"
   provision and, 21; impetus for, 22,
   30; individualist culture and, 19, 20;
   objectives of, 20; rules of, 20, 21;
   Work Pays and, 21
Iowa Test of Basic Skills, 90

Job Opportunities and Basic Skills (JOBS)
   Program, 28
Johnson, Lyndon B.: Great Society and,
   8; welfare reform and, 16
Johnson, Tom, 30

Kennedy, John F., 16
Krauss, Caroline, 30

labor force participation: depression and,
   82; descriptive statistics and, 68, 70;
   earnings and, 75; gender and effects
   of, 91, 92; long-term welfare and, 73,
   74; sanctions and, 103 and table 8.3;
   study design and, 66–67, 68. *See also*
   work
Land of Lincoln Legal Assistance
   Program, 28
Lang, Lou, 31
Legal Assistance Foundation, 28
liberals: AFDC and, 7; causes of poverty
   and, 114, 115; children and theories
   of, 87; context of competing
   paradigms, 126 fig. 10.2, 128; poverty
   theory and, 78; PRWORA effects
   and, 111; welfare and, 5, 6; welfare
   perspective, 127; welfare reform and,
   8, 123, 124 and fig. 10.1
litigation: welfare reform and, 28
Losing Ground (Murray), 17, 56, 110

Medicaid: increase in, 63; TANF
   recipients and, 58
mental health. *See* depression
Mulligan, Rosemary, 31
Murray, Charles: conservative answer
   and, 17, 97; Contract for America
   movement, 16; depression and
   poverty theory of, 78; long-term
   welfare and, 73

neighborhoods: characteristics of, 67;
   characteristics of Chicago, 118 and
   table 9.1; individual characteristics
   and odds of moving to, 119 table
   9.2; racial segregation and change of,

120 table 9.3; reasons to remain or
relocate and, 120–121
Nixon, Richard M., 16
nonwage income, 67

Obama, Barack, 5, 124

person-centered strategy: policy and,
10; response to reforms and, 36, 37;
welfare life, 125; welfare reform and,
12, 129
Personal Responsibility and Work
Opportunity Reconciliation Act
(PRWORA): accountability and, 19;
effects of, 126; Illinois poor and, 5, 6;
right of citizenship and, 7; work first
strategy and, 20
policy analysis: person-centered strategy
and, 10, 12; unimodality and, 9
Poor Support (Ellwood), 18, 110
poverty: African-American children and,
16; bad behaviors and, 8; behavioral
reactions to, 5; Chicago and decline
in, 117; factors of, 15; failure of
system and, 17; impact of PRWORA
on, 6; neighborhood and, 111, 112;
neighborhood characteristics and,
118 and table 9.1; QHWRA and, 115;
rates in Midwestern states, 23 fig. 2.1;
segregation and, 113, 114; values and,
18; welfare reform and, 76
PRWORA. See Personal Responsibility
and Work Opportunity Reconciliation
Act (PRWORA)

Quality Housing and Work
Responsibility Act (QHWRA), 115

Rauschenberger, Steve, 27, 31
Reagan, Ronald, 16
Republicans: Illinois welfare reform and,
30–32
Ronen, Carol, 30
Roosevelt, Franklin D., 8

sanctions: characteristics of recipients
and, 99 and table 8.1; effects of,
98, 99; material hardships and,
60, 61, 101 and table 8.2; personal
experiences of, 107–109; predictors
of, 101, 105 table 8.4, 106 table 8.4;
welfare exit and, 104
single-mother: households and, 15;

mental health treatment and, 78
socializing agent, 7
Springfield data collection, 131
state welfare policies: TANF programs
and, 19
Supplemental Security Income (SSI):
welfare-like program of, 26
Syverson, David, 30

t-tests, 134
Temporary Assistance for Needy Families
(TANF): accountability, 19; decrease
in caseloads and, 50–51, 52, 60 table
4.1; health problems and, 76; material
hardship and, 60 table 4.1; sanctions
and, 98
Tobit model, 67
Truly Disadvantaged (Wilson), 67, 113

unemployment: economic slowdown
and, 52
Unemployment Insurance system (UI),
14, 66, 100

welfare: depression and recipients of, 77;
long-term, 67, 68
welfare caseload study. See Illinois
Families Study (IFS)
welfare reform: child care and, 55, 56;
demographic variables and exit from,
102 table 8.3, 103 and table 8.3, 104;
disaffected and, 43–45; economic
inclusion and, 7; elimination of AFDC
and, 76; financial situation and, 56–
58, 59; impact on Chicagoans, 122;
individuals and, 8; individuals and
policies of, 128; non-working group
and, 64, 65; nurturers and, 38–39, 40,
53; objectives of, 27; person centered
research and, 129; political culture
and, 27, 28; private sector and, 128;
providers and, 40–42, 43, 50, 54, 58;
PRWORA and, 6; research policy and,
127–129; sanctions and, 59, 60, 61,
97–109; state imposed time limits
and, 16; work first strategy and, 30;
working group and, 63, 64. See also
Illinois Families Study (IFS)
Welfare Reform Research and
Accountability Act, 5, 7
Wilson, William Julius, 67
work: demographic characteristics of
IFS and, 64 table 4.2; depression and

importance of, 84; domestic violence and, 83; earnings and, 53–54, 55; IFS and trends in, 52 fig. 4.1; impact on academic achievement, 91, 92; influences on, 70, 73; log earnings and, 72 table 5.4; long-term, 71 table 5.3; longer periods of, 73, 74; material hardship and, 58, 59, 60 table 4.1, 61 fig. 4.3; stress and, 77; welfare status and, 70 table 5.2. See also labor force participation

Work Incentive (WIN) Demonstration Project, 28

Work Pays, 21